THE SILVER CORD

Buried in the Fat Portions of the Earth

Young Kim

**outskirts
press**

Outskirts Press, Inc.
http://www.outskirtspress.com

ISBN: 978-1-9772-4384-3

Scripture taken from The NIV Study Bible, Zondervan Publishing House

Outskirts Press and the "OP" logo are trademarks belonging to Outskirts Press, Inc.

PRINTED IN THE UNITED STATES OF AMERICA

TABLE OF CONTENTS

Chapter 1

———∿∿———

GOD & HIS CREATURE

Tears of God

- Joyful tears: Affluent rain producing a good harvest, like His lost peoples returning to Him through the Word and the Holy Spirit.

- Tears from anger: Still from His compassion, a flood of stormy rain to awake the lost from their deadly sleep in the poison of a sinful nature (fat portions).

- Tears dried out: The final judgment, fire due to severe drought; fire storms or disastrous fire, from either man's fault or natural disaster.

Genesis 9:13 "Never again will the waters become a flood to destroy all life." As long as God has tears, before His tears dry out completely, man is absolutely requested to awake from the deadly sleep in the poison of a sinful nature (fat portions).

The third revolt of "desire" in fat portions of man:

Genesis 3:4-6 "The desires for gaining wisdom to be like God has made three major revolts against God, the Creator, replacing God, the Creator with gods of the age, which is idolatry."

-The first revolt

"Have you eaten the tree that I commanded you not to eat from?" Genesis 3:11

-The second revolt

Then they said, "Come let us build ourselves a city with tower that reaches to the heavens—that is why it was called Babel." Genesis 11:4-9

-The third revolt

Man's attempt to make a copy of creation, including animals, and even man, which will be the greatest revolt man has ever made against God the Creator since His creation. Making robots or copying man, or performing a sex-change is an unforgivable challenge of defying God's probation to the fallen man. (Genesis 3:19) It goes against His salvation plan for man to lift the probation through the Word and Holy Spirit by destroying Satan by His grace, sending Jesus Christ, the Word, and the Holy Spirit.

-The first punishment

"So the Lord God banished them from Garden of Eden to work the ground from which he had been taken." (Genesis 3:23)

-The second punishment

"From there the Lord scattered them over the face of whole earth." (Genesis 11:8"

-The third punishment

"Woe to them!" (2 Timothy 3:1-4) "They have taken the way of Cain; they have rushed for profit into Balaam's error; they have been destroyed in Korah's rebellion." (Jude 11) "But the day of the Lord will come like a thief. The heavens will disappear with a roar; the element will be destroyed by fire and the earth and everything in it will be laid bare." (2 Peter 3:10.)

Chapter 2

―――∾∾――――

MAN'S OFFERING TO GOD

Abel's Offering, the Fat Portions
Man's Seminal Sins

Genesis 3:6

Good for food—unquenchable greed in a living paradise.

Pleasing to the eyes—sensual lust.

Evil desire—replacing God, the Creator with gods of this age and empty ambition, and elevating the level of the creatures to that of Creator.

By faith, Abel brought these fat portions for his offering to God from painful repentance in a broken spirit and contrite heart. (Interpreted from Hebrews 11:4)

The substance of the fat portion is necessary for man's existence to balance and rule over the other creatures as instincts (quoted Genesis 1:28). But when they are tempted by the work of Satan and fall, they become seminal sins from the substance for original function for man's existence. They are to be considered as part of God's creation, for God said, "All the fat is the Lord's." (Leviticus 3:16)

It appears more clearly in 1 John 3:8: "He who does what is sinful is of the devil, because the devil has been sinning from the beginning, the reason the Son of Man appeared was to destroy the devil's work."

2 Corinthians 5:17-19: "Therefore, if anyone is in Christ, he is a new creation; the old one has gone, the new one has come, all this is from God—not counting Man's sins against them."

God's salvation plan for man, by destroying Satan through the Word and the Holy Spirit by sending Jesus Christ, is deeply and directly related with Abel's offering the fat portions.

In the Old Testament, the first sin offering to God is Abel's offering of fat portions, which must have been burnt away on the altar. So the sinful nature of man must be burnt away or crucified by the fire of the Word and the Holy Spirit through Jesus Christ in the New Testament. See the following scriptures:

Genesis 4:4
Leviticus 3:16
Leviticus 4:31
Luke 3:16
Galatians 5:24
Romans 8:9-14,

… which describe the backbone of God's salvation plan for man.

Cain's Offering: Fruits
Satan's Bait

"The fruit of the tree was good for food and pleasing to the eye and also desirable for gaining wisdom." Genesis 3:6 was used as the bait of Satan, with which Satan tempted the first men and caused them to fall.

Cain brought to God for his offering Satan's bait, by which his parents were tempted and fell. God must have been disappointed with them, and they were rejected. Why is Cain's offering relevant to modern Christians?

Fat portions = sinful nature = seminal sins

Genesis 4:4
But Abel brought fat portions from some of the finest born of his flocks. Abel offered to God the fat portions of human's sinful nature, which is man's seminal sin, on behalf of his parents, with which they fell to Satan's temptation.

Genesis 3:6
Seminal sins; good for food—unquenched greed pleasing to the eye—sensual lust, desire—replacing God the Creator with worldly gods of the age, which is idolatry. Considering that the first men lived in a paradise where they had nothing to look for, man's seminal sins were on the horizon.

Leviticus 3:16
Burning fat portions—the priest shall burn them on the altar as food, an offering made by fire, a pleasing aroma. All the fat is the Lord's. This is a lasting ordinance: You must not eat any fat or blood. The odor from burning all fat portions was figuratively expressed. God is not a secular god, who takes pleasure in smelling burning animal fat.

Man's sinful nature:
Psalms 5:5
"Surely I was sinful at birth from the time when my mother conceived me."

Romans 7:24-25

"What a wretched man I am! Who will rescue me from this body of death. Thanks be to God—through Jesus Christ our Lord."

Psalms 5:10

"Create in me a pure heart. O God, and renew a steadfast spirit within me."

Abel brought the fat portions of the sinful nature for the sacrifice to God by faith that God would listen to his petition from his contrite and broken heart for the sins his parents had committed (inferred from Hebrews 11:4 and Psalms 51:16-17).

Psalms 51:16-17 (Sacrifice to God)

"You do not delight in sacrifice or I would bring it; you do not take pleasure in burnt offering. The sacrifices of God are a broken and contrite heart."

The sacrifices of God are the sinner's groaning from the sorrowful repentance by putting off a sinful nature in a broken and contrite heart through the fire of the Word and the Holy Spirit, which is a fragrance to God, figuratively expressed as an aroma from the burning animal fats.

Colossians 3:5-6

"Put to death, therefore, whatever belongs to your earthly nature; sexual immorality, impurity, lust, evil desire and greed, which is idolatry. Because of them, the wrath of God is coming."

All these are the principal products from man's sinful nature when it is targeted and triggered to man's sinful nature by Satan. God's salvation plan for man is the process to destroy the work of Satan (1 John 3:8) by burning away the fat portions—the sinful nature, the seminal sin with the Word and the Holy Spirit.

It is a long-term and painful process, but full of His grace.

An Aroma Pleasing to God
The Groaning of Sorrowful Repentance

Leviticus 4:31

"He shall remove all the fat, just as the fat is removed—and the priest shall burn it on the altar as an aroma pleasing to the Lord. In this way the priest will make atonement for him, and he will be forgiven."

Hebrews 12:6

"...because the Lord disciplines those He loves and he punishes everyone He accepts as a son."

Jesus Christ, the high priest in the New Testament who shed His blood for man's sin asks man to offer man's sinful nature (the fat portions Abel offered to God) to God and burn it away on the Cross "through which the world has been crucified to me, and I to the world" as Paul said in Galatians 6:14.

Further, He asks "to offer your bodies as living sacrifices, holy and pleasing to God" (Romans 12:1), which comes from the groaning repentance of the broken and contrite heart, which is an aroma, or a fragrance to God.

God, who is Creator of all things, including all kinds of fragrance, does not have a preference for the burning smell of animal fat. When man offers the fat portions of his sinful nature and burns them away with the Word and the Holy Spirit and buries even the ashes into the baptism of Jesus' death (Mark 10:39), he makes complete atonement to God. God takes the groaning of sorrowful repentance of the worst sinner from a broken and contrite heart as fragrant aroma and accepts him as a child of God, as long as he proves it by his way of living.

Chapter 3

GOD CANNOT BE CRUCIFIED

God is the Spirit. Jesus Christ, who was conceived of the Holy Spirit full divine (Matthew 1:20, Luke 1:35) who is over all God, cannot be crucified. Jesus Christ, who was born of the Virgin Mary, full human, was crucified. The Spirit who was alive in the dead body of Jesus Christ made Him resurrected and made Him full divine, the Son of God. (Romans 1:4)

Related scriptures:
Daniel 7:13-14
Isaiah 42:1,6
Isaiah 11:1-5
1 Peter 1:20; (chosen before the creation of the world), and Luke 9:35 ("This is my Son, whom I have chosen.")
Hebrews 1:4-5. 5:5-6
Psalms 2:7
Acts 13:23
John 12:49-50, 17:19, 24 (the glory, you have given me before the creation of the world).

Chapter 4

———❧———

GOD'S PLAN FOR MAN'S SALVATION

The Origin (Root) of God's Salvation Plan for Man and Its Reality

Genesis 3:6
"When the woman saw the fruit was good for food and pleasing to the eye; [lust]
and also desirable for gaining wisdom; [evil desire to be like God, the Creator]
she took some and ate it [greed].

The roots of sin are lust, greed, and evil desire, which are the fat portions of man. Abel offered the fat portions (Genesis 6:4) to God with a broken and contrite heart (Psalms 51:16-17), repenting the sins which his parents had committed due to this fat portions against God's command, living in the paradise where they didn't need anything except to observe God's one command not to eat from the tree of the knowledge of good and evil. Abel offered to God on behalf of his parents these fat portions, which man must not eat but must be burnt away. (Leviticus 3:16)

In the New Testament these fat portions were termed into the sinful nature on idolatry (Colossians 3:5); putting to death, therefore, whatever belongs to your earthly nature: sexual immorality, impurity, lust, evil desires, and greed, all of which are idolatry. God's ultimate salvation plan is to destroy Satan's work by burning away (controlling) these fat portions (sinful nature) by his Word and the Holy Spirit through Jesus Christ, which will eventually destroy the plan of Satan (1 John 3:8) from the believers, so that the Kingdom of God may be restored in the believers. (Matthew 12:28)

2 Corinthians 6:1-2
"We urge you not to receive God's grace in vain. For He says, 'In the time of my favor I heard you, and in the day of salvation I helped you.' I tell you, now is the time of God's favor, now is the time of salvation."

Unless you are born again (John 3:3-5), unless you have the kingdom of God (1 John 17:21), through resurrection in Jesus Christ in this present world, there will be neither resurrection nor the kingdom of God in the coming world.

The Greatest Plan of God

(In the image of God, in the likeness of God, Genesis 1:26 in the likeness of sinful man, Romans 8:3-4)

Job 1:6-13
"Then the Lord said to Satan, 'Have you considered my servant Job?'"
"Then the Lord said to Satan, 'Very well, then, everything he has is in your hands, but on the man himself do not lay a finger.'"

Matthew 4:1

Jesus was led by the spirit into the desert to be tempted by the devil. God allowed Satan to tempt or test Jesus in two major ways, explicitly, in the history of the struggle between God and Satan.

Genesis 3:4-8

"'You will not surely die,' the serpent said to the woman. 'For God knows that when you eat of it, you will be opened and you will be like God, knowing good and evil.'"

Almighty God is the Omniscient. It appears that the devil's temptation was allowed implicitly by God, according to the scriptures of 1 John 5:9, John 8:44, Ephesians 2:2, 2 Corinthians 3:4, Revelation 12:9, and John 12:31. Satan is powerful and even the chief of the fallen evil spirits, who has been the fatal adversary of God and man.

John 3:8-9

He who does what it sinful is of the devil because the devil has been sinning from the beginning. The reason the Son of Man appeared was to destroy the devil's work.

Luke 4:43, Matthew 12:28

"But He said, 'I must preach the good news of the kingdom of God to the other towns also, because that is why I was sent.'"

The reason God sent Jesus Christ to the world was to recover the Kingdom of God in the mind and the heart of His lost people by destroying the devil's work through the Word and the Holy Spirit.

Genesis 1:26

"Then God said, 'Let us make man in our image in our likeness.'"

Man was created not so perfect as not to be tempted by Satan, just in the likeness of God but vulnerable to Satan's temptation.

Question: How was God Almighty, the Omniscient, not aware of the first man to be tempted and to fall at Satan's temptation?
Yes, He was the Omniscient; He should have foreseen it.

Genesis 1:26
"And let them rule over all the creatures that move along the ground."

This verse implies that God did not want someone else, like Satan, to rule over His creatures, but rather, He wanted man to do this. It also suggests that Satan, who employed the crafty serpent to tempt the first man, had already been there before the creation of man. When God said, "Let them rule over all the creatures," didn't God have foreknowledge that Satan would intrude into His plan?
Yes, the Omniscient should have known it.

Question:
What was God's ultimate plan in His mind, and why?

Genesis 3:15
"He will crush your head."

1 John 3:9
The reason the Son of Man appeared was to destroy the devil's work.

Romans 16:20
The God of peace will soon crush Satan.

Revelation 20:10

"And the devil, who deceived them was thrown into the lake of burning sulfur."

His plan is to terminate Satan in the world of His creatures. Satan stepped into God's plan, as God planned, by tempting the first man, who was created vulnerable at Satan's temptation. Satan is blinded in nature by only immediate evil ambition to alienate man from God, although he is powerful and crafty in doing any evil.

"In the image of God, in the likeness of God" and "In the likeness of sinful man" are God's merciful and long-term plans to terminate Satan in the world of His creatures. Satan didn't have a hint about having stepped in His plan when Satan ventured to tempt the first man.

Question:
Why did God choose the painful and long-term plan, even though Almighty God could have destroyed Satan at once?

God's mercy is to be considered.

Satan's possible reckless and brutal resistance may inflict enormous damage to His creatures.

God's patience is aimed at saving as many as possible of His chosen people in coming generations.

Romans 8:3-4

"In the likeness of sinful man."

By sending His own son in the likeness of sinful man to be a sin offering, God condemned sin in the sinful nature.

John12:32

"Now is the time of judgment on this world; now the prince of this world will be driven out from the earth. But I, when I am lifted up from the earth, will draw all men to myself."

Romans 8:13-14
"…but if by the spirit you put to death the misdeeds of the body, you will live because those who are led by the Spirit of God are sons of God."

Revelation 12:11
"They overcame him (Satan) by the blood of lamb and by the Word of their testimony."

Satan realizes now, even if it is too late for him to withdraw, that he has already deeply stepped in God's plan and sees no way to make terms with God in His unchangeable determination to terminate Satan. Having seen that his final fate is on the horizon, he has been desperate to resort to all kinds of evil ways: conflicts, division, immoralism, terrorism, mass murder, casualties by gun violence. What is more vile and brutal, he is using people's mental illness to tempt them into gun violence.

God sent His Son in the likeness of sinful man to recover the kingdom of God to His lost peoples in the image of God, in the likeness to be like Him in true righteousness and holiness (Ephesians 4:24) by terminating Satan among His creatures through the Son, the Word, and the Holy Spirit. Jesus Christ, who was conceived of the Holy Spirit and born of the Virgin Mary, is full human and full divine. His full humanity was subject to His full divinity, which had kept Him entirely out of sin at any kind despite Satan's temptations.

"In the likeness of God" and "in the likeness of sinful man" can be said to be the backbone of God's salvation plan for man to terminate Satan from all His creatures.

Before creation of the world, as Jesus Christ was chosen, God's salvation plan for man must have been conceived to destroy Satan by the Word and the Holy Spirit through Jesus Christ.

1 John 3:8
He who does what it sinful is of the devil, because the devil has been sinning from the beginning. The reason the Son of God appeared was to destroy the devil's work.

Jesus Christ, after forty days of fasting, frustrated Satan's temptation, saying, "Man does not live by bread alone but every word that comes from the mouth of God." (Matthew 4:4)

Ephesians 6:14-18 talks about the full armor of God for the believers' struggle against those evil sinful things of the world and makes it clear that the only weapon for offense against those evil forces is the sword of God, which is the Word of God.

Matthew 12:28
"But I drive out demons by the Spirit of God, then the kingdom of God has come upon you."

The Spirit of God is the sword of God, which is the Word of God.

Mathew 21:31
"I tell you the truth, the tax collectors and the prostitutes are entering the Kingdom of God ahead of you."

The truth of God's salvation plan for man is that any man, Jew or Gentile, regardless of who he is, or what he is, if he takes His Word, repents, turns to God and proves repentance in his way of living, that man is the son of God entering the Kingdom of God, for whom God sent the Son and the Holy Spirit. That is His salvation plan for man.

Matthew 4:17
"Repent, for the kingdom of heaven is near."

The kingdom of God was just being inaugurated.

Matthew 4:23
Preaching the good news of the kingdom, the good news of the kingdom is Jesus Christ Himself, the Incarnate. As said in John 1:14, the Word became flesh and made His dwelling among us. The Word, which is dwelling among the believers, ushers in the kingdom of God through the Holy Spirit.

"The kingdom of God is within you." (Matthew 17:21)

Chapter 5

MOSES'S VISION OF THE
KINGDOM OF GOD

Deuteronomy 8:1-3

"Be careful to follow every command I am giving to you today, so that you may live and increase and may enter the Lord promised on earth to your forefathers. Remember how the Lord your God led you all the way in the desert these forty years, to humble you and to test you in order to know what was in your heart, whether or not you would keep his command. He humbled you, causing you to hunger and then feeding you with manna, which is neither you nor your forefathers had known, to teach you that man does not live on bread alone but on every word that comes from the mouth of the Lord."

Major issues that are interrelated:

- Entering the land God promised—the kingdom of God

- God's harsh training and testing to humble as to accept and keep the Word

- Jesus' sufferings and the believers' sharing them through the baptism of death.

- The ultimate weapon to go through to the promised land (the kingdom of God) is the Word.

Moses visualized vividly God's salvation plan through His Word, the Incarnate, Jesus Christ, which would happen around one thousand five hundred years later in the New Testament, as God's forty-year training of the Israelites in the desert was to humble them by keeping His Word in order for them to enter the promised land. In the New Testament, believers' sharing in Jesus' sufferings to become like Him in His death, putting off the old self and putting on the new self with the Word and the Holy Spirit, makes it possible for the believers to enter the kingdom of God.

Genesis 3:19-20
"By the sweat of your brow, you will eat your food until you return to the ground, since from it you were taken and to dust you will return; it is God's probation to the fallen men."

Everyone has to do hard work to get an earthly living, to be spoiled by eating after a while.

But every Word that comes from the mouth of God, which is free of charge, gives eternal life, enduring forever.

The Word is God's grace for man, through which man is to be lifted from probation, and the Word is the key to the kingdom of God by being born again through faith in the power of God, who raised Jesus Christ from the dead. By the Word, the body of the mortal, destined to return to dust, is swallowed up to be immortal, to be like Jesus Christ through repenting, turning to God, and proving repentance by living, which leads to holiness, and righteousness, and resurrection in Jesus Christ for the kingdom of God. The first prophet of God was telling the kingdom of God through the Word, the Incarnate, Jesus Christ.

Chapter 6

———— ⧢ ————

THE LORD'S PRAYER

The Lord's Prayer
(The Kingdom of God)

Matthew 6:9

The tense is in the form of the present. There is neither the past nor distinction between the present and future, which is one in God. The sinful past has been erased away, by and with the grace of God.

The kingdom of God comes to the born-again believer when the Holy name of God is upheld holy, and His Holy name is known in the world by the believer's becoming holy, as he is born again to be holy in His holiness. (Leviticus 11:44-45; Luke 17:21).

The will of God is to be done accordingly among the believers, in the world, in whom the kingdom of God is established through the born-again. (John 3:3-5)

The will of God is His salvation plan for man through the Son, Jesus Christ, and He confirms that "Man does not live bread alone, but on every word that comes from the mouth of God." (Matthew 4:4)

He needs the Word every day to take up his cross daily, as much as physical foods, in order to sustain the kingdom of God in him. The born-again believer who is to be—by the revelation of God that is the Word and the Holy Spirit—realizes that there is nothing not to forgive as he reflects his past sinful life to be forgiven by the grace of God. And he comes to admit that all things have been done and also will be done according to His plan, which is in His providence.

Man is tempted by his sinful nature, which allows to commit sins of evil, and when it is full-grown it gives birth to death. (James 1:15)

Therefore, the root of evil, which is the sinful nature, is to be fired and burnt away by the Word and the Holy Spirit, which sustains the kingdom of God in the believer.

He acknowledges that the kingdom of God, His power, and His Glory are forever and ever.

Chapter 7

―――∼∽∼―――

THE LOVE OF GOD
FROM HIS GRACE

The Love of God

Genesis 3:21-23

"The Lord God made garments of skin for Adam and his wife and clothed them and the Lord God said, 'The man has now become more like one of us knowing good and evil. He must not be allowed to reach out his hand and take also from the tree of life and eat, and live forever.' So the Lord God banished him from the Garden of Eden to work the ground from which he had been taken."

God still didn't condemn them but gave a probation for the sin they had committed. Instead, He showed mercy by making garments of skin for Adam and his wife and clothing them, which signifies His intention to restore them and somehow to reach the tree of life according to His salvation plan through Jesus Christ, who is the tree of life.

Ezekiel 34:16

"I will search for the lost and bring the strays."

Matthew 18:14

"In the same way your father in heaven is not willing that any of the little ones should be lost."

Luke 15:4-7

"I tell you that in the same way there will be more rejoicing in heaven over one sinner who repents than over ninety-nine righteous who do not need to repent."

Luke 19:10

"For the Son of Man came to seek what was lost."

Luke 15:6

"Rejoice with me; I have found my lost sheep."

John 3:16

For God so loved the world that He gave his one and only Son, that whoever believes in Him shall not perish but have eternal life. For God did not send His Son into the world to condemn the world, but to save the world through Him.

"Whoever believes in Him who is the tree of life" is the gracious proposition of God for the sinners to lift up the probation. "Whoever believes in Him will not perish but have eternal life" is God's salvation, not only lifting up the probation but giving eternal life.

John 4:8-10

God is love. This is how God showed His love among us. He sent His one and only Son into the world, that He might love through Him. This is love: not that we loved God, but God loved us and sent His Son as an anointing sacrifice for our sins.

Romans 8:30
"Those He justified, He also glorified."

God justifies those who have faith in Jesus Christ, and those He justifies He makes born again, sanctified, and reconciled in Jesus Christ through His Spirit to become His children.

God came on the earth taking the form of humanity in Jesus Christ to seek and save His lost ones. He is working to restore the lost to be like Himself in His true righteousness and holiness, so that they may be like children of God in the order of Jesus Christ.

What an amazing thing the love of God is!

Grace of God #1

Romans 5:20
"Where sin increased, grace increased all the more, just as sin reigns in death so also grace might reign through righteousness to bring eternal life."

Those who seek God in broken spirit, with a broken and contrite heart from great repentance for grave sins committed in the past may experience the grace of God as it is, appreciating it more realistically, which makes them transformed or born again.

They surrender themselves completely to Jesus Christ, putting off the old self and putting on a new self, which allows the Holy Spirit to work through the Word in them, and moves them to devote their lives to the Lord:

-The sinful woman (Luke 7: 36-50, Matthew 26: 6-13) anointed Jesus Christ with expensive oil. Jesus said her devotion will be told along with His teaching.

-James, Jesus' half-brother who did not believe in Jesus Christ, and opposed Him, risked his life to be His witness and wrote the Book of James in the New Testament.

-Peter Simon, who disowned Jesus three times facing fearful situations, wrote the two books of 1 Peter and 2 Peter in the New Testament and was crucified for the Lord.

-Paul, who persecuted Jesus' followers exhaustively and witnessed at Timothy's death, called himself the worst sinner of sinners and risked his entire life for the Cause of Jesus Christ. He wrote thirteen books of Epistles in the New Testament and became the Apostle of Gentiles. He established the doctrine of justification by faith; the righteousness from God comes through justification by faith in Jesus Christ.

Through the grace of God in the Word and the Holy Spirit by sending Jesus Christ, from which salvation comes to those who believe in Jesus Christ through repentance, turning to God and proving the repentance by living, God uses them according to His purpose regardless of how grave the sins are that they had committed in the past.

Grace of God #2 /The Silver Cord of God
The Gracious God Whom I Met in a Bowl of Oatmeal Gruel

When I was ten years old, our family came to Busan, South Korea during the Korean War, having boarded an American warship with many other refugees who faced an immediate threat of persecution by the communists when they recaptured the city of Wonsan, North Korea. Our desperate, life-or-death situation was beyond description.

We left our hometown where our ancestors had lived for more than 300 years, covered with blazing fire and smoke, coupled with heavy gunfire, in the dark evening of early winter. As soon as we arrived in Busan, South Korea overnight, we were to stay in two separate refugee camps. After three days, we were forced out. Most people who did not have any relatives in Busan proceeded to the small mountain town of Yongdoosan.

Our family was me, my mother, my three elder sisters, and one elder brother. Our ages ranged from ten to nineteen. I was the youngest, without a father. He died when I was three years old.

We set up a temporary shelter with rice bags made of straw on the face of the mountain. Busan, located at the end of the south Korean Peninsula, has a mild winter. But it was pretty cold and windy on the mountain, and overnight our toes and fingertips became frostbitten. While sleeping at night, I used to awaken because wild rats were biting my fingers for something to eat.

Our one meal a day at home was watery gruel with a little bit of barley at home. I can't find any words to describe the miserable situation at that time. The only aid organization was the Red Cross, which served oatmeal gruel to the children for a lunch once a day. The personnel made oatmeal gruel by pouring dry milk powder and oatmeal into boiling water in big iron pot. So many kids lined up well before noon with a small aluminum bowl, waiting for their turn. The wonderful taste remains vivid in my memory. Its taste was better than a king's banquet to me.

I happened to ask the Red Cross personnel where it came from. He said it came from a country where Christians sent aid to help the poor.

This motivated me to find the God whom I met in the bowl of oatmeal gruel, and I attended a Sunday school without any absences, as a model kid. I participated in every contest of Bible recitals, winning prizes, until I drifted away from God because of two failures to be admitted to the school I wanted to get into, at the ages of thirteen and nineteen. My failures caused me unforgettable anguish, because the direction of my life was forced to change.

At the age of thirty-three, in the midst of the rise and fall in my life, I came to Chicago, which was my third visit to the USA, and opened a wholesale business, acting as a branch office of an export company in Korea where I worked for some years.

The God whom I met in the bowl of oatmeal gruel at the age of ten has kept track of me and led me to attend a small Korean immigrants' church. He made me devout and taught me what it meant to be devoted to God as my business was growing.

Unfortunately, I fell victim to Satan and was plunged into turmoil at the age of thirty-eight. I have experienced thoroughly how grave the consequences of sin are, having failed to love God with all my heart, all my soul, all my strength, and all my mind (Matthew 22:37, Mark 12:30) and having failed to love my neighbor as myself, forgetting Paul's saying "love does no harm to its neighbor." (Romans 13:10)

In such harsh struggles against the consequences of my sin, my gracious God called me again, having picked my soul from the muddy pit by reaching out His hands. He made it possible for me to graduate from The Moody Bible Institute in 2011 at the age of seventy-one. But He has been chastising me and my surroundings so that I might repent thoroughly from all kinds of sins I had committed for my lifetime, pouring tears from a broken and contrite heart. Sometimes He awoke me from my sleep and reminded me of even trivial sins, which I did not fail to repent of, as He led me. Yet He does not stop to awake me.

On the early morning of my 74th birthday, I was awakened again but was blessed to confess my faith by the grace of God the Father whom I met in the aluminum bowl of oatmeal gruel at the age of ten. This is faith from the Word, participating in Jesus' baptism of death, taking off the old self and putting on new self through the fire of the Word and the Holy Spirit, born again sanctified, and resurrected in Jesus Christ with redemption of the body, the children of God, the kingdom of God, eternal life.

God has made me realize that the silver cord of God the Father has been bound around my waist from the time my mother conceived me, and He has tracked me throughout the rise and fall of my life.

God works good in all things for those who love Him, who have been called according to His purpose. (Romans 8:28)

Throughout all the failures and success of His lost people in this world, God leads them to the goal of reaching the kingdom of God, which is the grace of God.

"Who is this that darkens my counsel with the words without knowledge?"
(Job 38:2)

This verse is God's response to Job out of the storm, when Satan drove Job into a corner, expecting that he would not refrain from cursing God, as Satan was so confident that Job would do. But Job did not curse God directly in such a horrible situation; instead he cursed his birth, not realizing that his birth was also given by God.

This grave question, "Who is this that darkens my counsel?" is to Satan, who had darkened God's counsel by saying to the first man in Genesis 3:4-5 "You will not surely die, for God knows that when you eat of it, your eyes will be opened and you will be like God, knowing good and evil," and who also challenged God to test his faithful servant with such horrible tests.

Therefore, God sent Jesus Christ to destroy the work of Satan from the beginning up to now, as Jesus said 1 John 3:8, "Because the devil has been sinning from the beginning, the reason the Son of God appeared was to destroy the devil's work."

This verse of Job 38:2 is also God's warning to all men as well.

How are we to interpret what is happening between God and Satan in Job 1:6-12? It can be construed as God's predeclaration of His plan to terminate Satan by sending the Word of living God, through Jesus Christ.

Chapter 8

JESUS CHRIST FROM HIS BIRTH,
SUFFERINGS, AND RESURRECTION

The Word

Genesis 1:1,3

"In the beginning God created the heaven and the earth, and a spirit of God was hovering in the water...and God said 'Let there be ____,'" ____

Psalms 32:16

"By the Word of the Lord were the heavens made..."

John 1:1

"In the beginning was the Word, and the Word was with God, and the Word was God."

Matthew 4:4

"Man does not live on bread alone but every word that comes from God..."

John 1:14

"The Word became flesh and made His dwelling among us…"

John 6:69

"You have the words of eternal life. We believe and know that you are the holy one of God."

2 Timothy 3:16

"All scripture is God breathed and useful _____, so that the man of God may be thoroughly equipped for every good work."

James 1:18

"He chose to give us birth through the word of truth…"

John 8:30

"If you obey my teaching, you are really my disciples, then you will know truth, the truth will set you free."

The word inspired by the Spirit of God who created the heaven and the earth by saying "let there be _____" was the Word with God in the beginning, and the Word was God. The Word, the second person of the Trinity, made His dwelling among us as the Word had to do with the original creation, so the same Word was with the new creation.

In the Old Testament, the Word was proclaimed either directly from the Lord or the prophets, while in the New Testament it was proclaimed through Jesus Christ in the spirit. The Word through which God created from nothing into being, and the same Word which gives birth to new life, has been sustaining all the creatures moving in the way according to his providence.

Romans 10:17

Consequently, faith comes from hearing the message, and the message is heard through the Word of Christ.

When a seed of the Word is fully grown, it gives birth to faith; when the faith is fully grown, it gives birth to new birth. The new birth through "continuous faith, established and firm, not moved from the hope held out in the gospel. This is the gospel, of which I, Paul, have become a servant" (Colossians 1:23) reaches the children of God, the redemption of the body.

Ephesians 6:17
"And the sword of the spirit, which is the Word of God..."
John 6:63
"The Spirit gives life; the words I have spoken to you are spirit and they are life."
Hebrews 4:12
"For the word of God is living and active. Sharper than any double-edged sword, it penetrates even dividing soul and spirit, joints and marrow, it judges and attitudes."

Therefore, the Word requests us to repent and prove repentance by living, which dictates those to be baptized with Jesus to be buried with Him "into the baptism of death" (Romans 6:3) and to be buried with Him in baptism and raised with Him "through faith in the power of God, who raised Him from the dead" (Colossians 2:12) and that the Word commands you to love your God with all your heart and soul and with all your mind and all your strength. The second is this: "Love your neighbor as yourself; there is no commandment greater than this." (Mark 30-31)

The faith from the Word is expressed itself through love. Galatians

5:6 says that those who love God and neighbor in such ways do not commit sin.

Luke 6:37-38
"Do not judge, and you will not be judged. Do not condemn, and you will not be condemned. Forgive, and you will be forgiven."

Luke 4:43
"I must preach the kingdom of God, because that is why I was sent; the Words to the kingdom of God."

Acts 1:3
"After His suffering, he showed himself to those men and gave many convincing proofs that He was alive. He appeared to them over a period of forty days and spoke about the kingdom of God."

The Word is condensed to give birth to new creation for loving God more than anything else in this world and your neighbor as yourself, by forgiving one another whatever grievances you may have (Colossians 3:13) to do good work (2 Timothy 3:16), focusing on the kingdom of God through resurrection in Jesus Christ, to make us children of God for Eternity. The farewell words of Jesus Christ to His disciples were the words of teaching the kingdom of God through resurrection.

We see in Jesus Christ, who is the Incarnate, the way of the born-again, through redemption of the body, the children of God, resurrection in Jesus Christ, the kingdom of God, the eternity, which is the gospel of good news through Jesus Christ to share with all nations.

-Resurrection -
God's grace was to have Jesus Christ become the Son of God by His resurrection, and His believers became children of God.

Romans 1:4

"And who through the Spirit of holiness was declared with power to be the Son of God by His resurrection from the dead: Jesus Christ our Lord."

Jesus Christ has become the Son of God as said in Acts13:33,"He has fulfilled for us, their children, by raising of Jesus." As it is written in the second Psalm: "You are my Son; today I have become your Father." Without resurrection, even Jesus Christ could not be conceivably become the Son of God.

Romans 4:25

"He was delivered over to death and raised to life for our justification."

By being resurrected, He ascended into heaven and sits at the right hand of God Almighty as Messiah. The King of kings, the Lord of the lords will come to judge the living who were justified and resurrected in Him, and He will judge the dead who sinned at the appointed time God has set with His own authority.

-Resurrection to the believers

When Jesus Christ gave Himself up for us as a fragrant offering and sacrifice to God (Ephesians 5:2), He became Jesus Christ (Messiah) by having believers become born again, resurrected in Him as He was raised from the dead. As said in Philippians 3:10, "...and the fellowship of sharing in His sufferings, becoming like Him in his death, and somehow to attain to the resurrection."

By sharing in His sufferings and becoming like Him in His death, we may be resurrected in Him, as said Romans 6:5-6, "If we have been united with Him like this in his death, we will be certainly also be united in His resurrection."

In Mark10:39 Jesus said, "You will drink a cup I drink and be baptized with the baptism I am baptized with."

John 6:5-4
"Whoever eats my flesh and drinks my blood has eternal life, and I will raise him on the last day."

-The resurrection in Jesus Christ makes possible for believers to enter the kingdom of God when they take the same steps as Jesus Christ took for us, taking off the old self and putting on the new self, which is becoming "born again" for the kingdom of God.

Luke 17:21
"Nor will people say, 'here it is,' or 'there it is,' because the kingdom of God is within you."

The resurrection in Jesus Christ through being born again delivers the believers to the kingdom of God; the kingdom of God is to be built in them before they leave the present world, "for which they should live this world as a stranger, for the kingdom of God is not of this world." (Matthew 18:36)

The day being of "born again" for resurrection is more blessed than the day of physical birth from the mother, because "born of sin" has become "born of the Spirit."

Easter Sunday Morning 3-27-16
The Resurrection (2)

Ephesians 4:24

"…and to put on the new self, created to be like God in true righteousness and holiness."

If man is recreated by recovering the image of God in their likeness of true righteousness and holiness as created by God, the Trinity (Genesis 1:27), man is to see and meet the God of the Trinity in His power of creation, His kingdom, His eternal power, His sovereignty and His Glory from His revelation of the Word and all the creations of the universe, which is the resurrection for the kingdom of God.

God sent, for this purpose, Jesus Christ, who has "become for us the wisdom from God, that is our righteousness, holiness, and redemption (1 Corinthians 1:29), which comes from man's sharing in His suffering, becoming like Him (in His righteousness and holiness) in His death, and somehow attaining to the resurrection." (Philippians 3:10-11) "In the likeness of God" is "In true righteousness and holiness."

Therefore, man's resurrection in Jesus Christ gives birth to new creation redeemed by Him. the old one has gone, the new one has come. All this is from God. (2 Corinthians 5:17-18)

Therefore, the cross for man to carry on earth, which is the yoke on his neck and the load on his back, is to bear up every day (Luke 9:23) as well as in the heart, not for the pleasure of the sinful nature, but for the sake of the resurrection, by recovering true righteousness and holiness to be like God in His likeness.

Who Is Jesus Christ? #1

- Before His birth: the Son of man

Daniel 7:13-14

"In my vision at night I looked, and there before me was one like a Son of Man, coming with clouds of heaven. He approached the Ancient of Days and was led into His presence. He was given authority, Glory and sovereign power; all peoples, nations, and men of every language worshipped him. His dominion is an everlasting dominion that will not pass away, and his kingdom is one that will never be destroyed."

The title of the Son of Man is the one He used for His identity; He who was created before the creation of the world for our sake, and who was born of Virgin Mary as a full man.

1 Peter 1:20-21
"He was chosen before the creation of the world, but was revealed in their last times for your sake, through Him you believe in God, who raised Him from the dead and glorified Him and so your faith and hope are in Him."

The grace of God was revealed to send the Son of Man, who was created before the creation of the world, according to His salvation plan for man.

-His birth: the Son of God and the Son of Man
Matthew 1:20-21
"Because what is conceived in her is from the Holy Spirit, because He will save His people from sins."

Luke 1:35
" 'The Holy Spirit will come upon you, and the Most High will over-shadow you. So the Holy One to be born will be called the Son of God.'"

Matthew 1:23

"The virgin will be with child and will give birth to a Son, and they will call Him the Immanuel—which means God with us."

John 1:1,10

"The Son of God who was conceived of the Holy Spirit was full divine, who had been with God in the beginning, who is the Word and became flesh and made His dwelling among us." "Who will be with us in His Word forever, Immanuel."

The Son of Man who was created before the creation of the world was born of Virgin Mary. Therefore Jesus Christ is full divine and full human.

God sent Him in the likeness of sinful man for the sacrifice of atonement for human sins, and so He condemned sins in sinful man, in order that the righteous requirements of the law might be fully met in us, who do not live according to the sinful nature but according to the spirit. (Romans 8:3-4)

-Jesus's sufferings for man's sins foretold
Isaiah 53:2-10

"...surely he took up our infirmities and carried our sorrows, yet we considered him stricken by God, smitten by Him, and afflicted. But he was pierced for our transgressions, he was crushed for our iniquities; the punishment that brought us peace was upon to him, and by his wounds we are healed."

His suffering on behalf of man is according to God's plan to recover the kingdom of God to His lost peoples through Him who transforms the worst sinners, turning to God through repenting from a broken and contrite heart. The process is the forgiveness of sins, being born again, and resurrection in Jesus Christ by following in His steps.

(Mark 10:39, Luke 3:16, Luke 9:23, Matthew 10:38, 16-24, Mark 8:34, Philippians 3:10-11, Ephesians 4:24, Romans 6:2-7, Colossians 3:5-6, Galatians 5:24)

-Jesus' resurrection
Romans 1:3-4
The gospel He promised beforehand through the prophets in the Holy Spirit regarding His Son, who as to human nature was a descendant of David, and through the Spirit of Holiness was declared with power to be the Son of God by His resurrection from the dead: Jesus Christ our Lord.

Acts 13:33-35, Hebrews 5:5
"He said to me, 'You are my Son; today I have become your Father.'"
"I will give you the holy and sure blessing promised to David."
"You will not your Holy One see decay." (Acts 2:27)

1 Peter 3:18
"He was put to death in the body, but made alive by the Spirit."

The Spirit, who was alive in Jesus' dead body, made Him resurrected in the incruciable and heavenly body. Jesus Christ, who was created before the creation of the word was born, for our sake (1 Peter 1:23), of the Virgin Mary and was crucified and was raised by the Spirit (Romans 1:4) who overwhelmed Mary at the conception of Jesus Christ.

"You are my Son; today I have become your Father." (See Matthew 1:20-21, 23; Luke1:35, Romans 1:4, Hebrews 5:5)

Jesus Christ ascended into heaven and sits at the right hand of the Father and will come to judge the living and the dead (as quoted in the Apostle's Creed)

-Jesus' ultimate teaching is the kingdom of God through resurrection (Matthew 4:17, Acts 1:3, Luke 17:20)

-Jesus commanded:
Matthew 28:19-20 - The great mission
Acts 1:8 - The great witness

Who Is Jesus Christ? #2
("You are my Son; today I have become your Father.")

Psalms 2:7
"I will proclaim the Decree of the Lord;
"He said to me 'You are my Son; today I have become your Father.'"

Acts 13:32-33
"We tell you the good news: what God promised our fathers He has fulfilled for us, their children, by raising Jesus. As it is written in the second psalm; 'You are my Son; today I have become your Father.'"

Romans 1:2-4
"The gospel He promised beforehand through His prophets in the Holy Scriptures regarding His Son, who as to human nature was a descendant of David, and through the Spirit of the holiness was declared with power to be the Son of God by His resurrection from the dead; Jesus Christ our Lord."

The scriptures of Romans 1:2-4 are considered a condensed summary regarding who Jesus Christ is:

-A descendant of David: the Son of Man born of the Virgin Mary
-The work of the Holy Spirit of whom He was conceived and who resurrected Him from the dead.
-The Son of God by His resurrection from the dead of the Son of Man, Jesus Christ our Lord.
-The Son of Man: the title Jesus used for Himself.
-Daniel 7:13-14

A Son of Man, coming with the clouds of heaven. He approached the Ancient of Days and was led into His presence. He was given authority, Glory, and sovereign power.

Isaiah 53:12
"Therefore I will give him a portion among the great, and he will divide the spoils with the strong, because he poured out his life into death, and was numbered with the transgressor. For he bore the sin of many, and made intercession for the transgressors."

Luke 22:37
" 'It is written: And he was numbered with the transgressors' - yes, what is written about me is reaching its fulfillment.'"

1 Peter 1:20
"He was chosen before the creation of the world, but was revealed in these last times for your sake. The Son of Man who was created before the creation of the world was born of the Virgin Mary, and was sent in the likeness of the sinful man to be a sin offering by God." (Romans 8:3)

The Son of God

Isaiah 42:1-3

"Here is my servant, whom I uphold, my chosen one in whom I delight; I will put my Spirit on Him and He will bring justice to the nations."

Matthew 1:20-22

"...because what is conceived in her is from the Holy Spirit. She will give birth to a Son, and you are to give Him the name Jesus, because He will save his people from their sins. All this took place to fulfill what the Lord had said through the prophet. The virgin will be with child and will give birth to a Son, and they will call him Immanuel, which means 'God with us.'"

Jesus, who was conceived of the Holy Spirit, was full divine was given all authority and sovereign power, which kept Him from any temptation of Satan and raised Him from the dead and made possible the resurrection for His believers.

1 Peter 3:18

"He was put to death in the body but made alive by the Spirit."

The Son of Man, who had been chosen by God before creation of the world, was born of the Virgin Mary, and was crucified and buried. Jesus Christ, who was conceived of the Holy Spirit, was not crucified. He was alive in Him from birth, during His public life, suffering, and death, having kept Him in divinity at any temptation of Satan.

The Son of God who was conceived of the Holy Spirit can't be crucified.

The Son of Man chosen by God, born of the virgin Mary, was crucified but resurrected by the power of the Spirit alive in Him, who was with Him by incarnation from His mother's womb and stayed with Him in His suffering and resurrection to His ascending, having kept the Son of Man in His divinity, and He became the Son of God by His resurrection. Jesus Christ conceived of the Holy Spirit who is God and cannot be crucified. He was alive in the dead body of Jesus Christ in the form of the Spirit, and also is in the resurrected body, indestructible as One of the Holy One, who ascended and sits at right hand of God the Father. He will come to judge the living and the dead. (Mark 14:62, Psalms 110:1, Daniel 7:14)

Jesus' resurrected body is not the body of the Virgin Mary, but the body of an indestructible life. (Hebrews 7:16-17)

He is the resurrection and life (John 11:25), with His Divine body.

He taught us what to do for our sin. We don't have to shed blood for our sin anymore, because a sacrifice of atonement to God is enough with that of Jesus Christ, His only Son. (John 3:16)

The faith which comes from the Word, inspired by the Holy Spirit, leads the believers to be baptized into His death and to be buried with Him through baptism into death in order that just as Jesus Christ was raised from the dead through the Glory of the Father, we too may have new life (Romans 6:3-4), and also said as in Colossians 2:11.

"In him you were also circumcised, in putting off the sinful nature, not with a circumcision done by the hands of men but with the circumcision done by Christ, having buried with Him in baptism and raised with Him through your faith in the power of God, who raised Him from the dead" through which the participants in Jesus' baptism of death will somehow attain to the resurrection (Philippians 3:10-11) and created to be like God in His righteousness and holiness (Ephesians 4:22-24).

This is offering the believer's body as a living and pleasing sacrifice to God (Romans 12:1). "Sacrifice and offering you did not desire, but a body you prepared for me." (Hebrews 10:5). Jesus Christ, as a firstborn among many brothers, opened the way to the believers' resurrection and the kingdom of God, which was His main teaching during His earthly life as well as after His resurrection, over a period of forty days (Acts 1:3), leaving the great mission of Matthew 28:19-20 and Hosea 24:47, Acts 1:8, and Mark 16:15-17.

The Greatest Miracle Jesus Performed for Man

Luke 4:43
"I must preach the good news of the kingdom of God in the other towns also, because this is the reason I was sent."

The good news is the gospel, and the gospel is the good news of the kingdom of God.

John 3:2-6
"He [Nicodemus] came to Jesus at night and said, 'Rabbi, we know that you are a teacher who has come from God. For no one could perform the miraculous signs you are doing if God were not with him.' In reply, Jesus declared, 'I tell you the truth, no one sees the kingdom of God unless he is born again.' 'How can a man be born again when he is old?' Nicodemus asked. 'Surely he cannot enter a second time into mother's womb to be born.' Jesus answered, 'I tell you the truth, no one can enter the kingdom of God unless he is born of water and a Spirit. Flesh gives birth to flesh, but the Spirit gives birth to Spirit."

When Nicodemus spoke in verse 2, Jesus awoke him, implying the greatest (real) miracle is being "born again." In verse 4, Jesus confirmed that a second time to be born through mother's womb is impossible. In verses 5 and 6, Jesus told the truth, that being "born again" is not through the mother's womb, but by the Spirit, which transforms the old one into the new one making an entire new creation of the body as well as the spirit, which are "born again."

John 3:8
He who does what it sinful is of the devil, because the devil has been sinning from the beginning. The reason the Son of God appeared was to destroy the devil's work.

Matthew 12:28
"And if I drive out demons by the Spirit of God, the kingdom of God has come upon you."

Jesus Christ clarified that He came to destroy the devil's work, which is the root of man's fall, by the Spirit of God and the Word.

Acts 1:3-4
"After His suffering, He showed Himself to these men and gave many convincing proofs that He was alive. He appeared to them over a period of forty days and spoke about the kingdom of God."

In closing His sojourn on earth, right before ascending to God, the Father, His final teaching was the kingdom of God through resurrection in Him, as it was at the launching of His earthly ministry. (Matthew 4:17)

Man is to pursue the way to the kingdom of God every day through the Word and the Holy Spirit as if today were the last day in this world before the day of Jesus' second coming, as Jesus directed us in Luke 17:21, through being born again—resurrection in Him.

Being born again through resurrection in Him is the greatest miracle Jesus has performed for man and the reason He came, which man is to experience before he leaves this world.

Jesus' crucifixion dictated the believers' redemption of the body.

Romans 8:23-24

"…not only so, but we ourselves, who have the first fruits of the Spirit, groan inwardly as we wait eagerly for our adoption as sons, the redemption of our bodies. For in this hope we were saved; the redemption of the body as adoption of son of God is the last stage to enter the Kingdom of God, which is the resurrection in Jesus Christ."

How can this happen?

John 6:5

"I tell you the truth. No one can enter the kingdom of God unless he is born of water and the Spirit."

John 6:7

"You must be surprised at my saying: 'You must be born again.'"

Romans 6:3

"Or don't you know that all of us who were baptized into Christ Jesus were baptized into His death? We were therefore buried with Him through the baptism of death in order that just as Christ was raised from the dead through the Glory of the Father, we too may live a new life."

Philippians 3:10-11

"I want to know Christ and the Power of His resurrection and the fellowship of sharing in His sufferings, becoming like Him in His death, and so somehow, to attain to the resurrection from the dead."

Mark 10:39

"Jesus said, 'You will drink the cup I drink and be baptized with the baptism I am baptized with.'"

Colossians 2:12

"Having been buried with Him in baptism and raised with Him through your faith in the Power of God, who raised Him from the dead."

Romans 8:17

"...if indeed we share in His sufferings in order that we may also share in His Glory."

Being born again, new life, (resurrection) redemption of body and the kingdom of God are to be done by the baptism of death, which is the product from the power of the Word through faith and the Spirit (Holy Spirit) of God.

The faith from the Word and the Holy Spirit enables the believers to participate in Jesus' sufferings, burning away the sinful nature with its practices, and burying even the ash of them into the death of Jesus Christ, which makes the redemption of the body.

Therefore, Jesus' crucifixion on the Cross presents dual supreme themes: the penalty to God on behalf of man to reconcile them to Him, and dictating them to attain the redemption of the body by putting off the old self and "putting on the new self, created to be like God in His righteousness and Holiness" (Ephesians 4:20), and offering to God "offering their bodies as living sacrifice, holy and pleasing to God (Romans 12:1).

Romans 8:24

"For in this hope we were saved."

We who were saved by Jesus' crucifixion are recreated to be like God in true righteousness and Holiness by putting on a new self through the Word and the Holy Spirit (Ephesians 4:24) to have ultimate hope to become children of God, which is the way to the kingdom of God through resurrection in Jesus Christ.

Jesus' Purpose and How to Accomplish It on Earth

-Recovering the kingdom of God to the believers along with resurrection through repentance from a broken and contrite heart, which is to be proved by deeds.
-Destroying two monstrous objects which have been against the Will of God:

- The devil, which has been sinning from the beginning.

- The sinful nature (fat portions) which have been the bait to the devil, which have caused man to fall.

-Destroying them by the Word and the Holy Spirit, which brings about "the kingdom of God within you" (Luke 17:21) and "our adoption as, the redemption of bodies." (Romans 8:23)

Related Scriptures:
Matthew 4:17, 4:1-10, Luke 3:16, Luke 11-20, Matthew 12:28, Luke 4:43, Ephesians 6:17, Titus 3:5-7, James 1:18, Romans 8:11, 13-14, John 1:14, John 3:8, 1 Peter 1:23, John 6:54, John 14:16, John 17:17, John 16:7-11

The Way

Matthew 4:17

"From that time on Jesus began to preach 'Repent, for the kingdom of God is near.'"

The main teaching of Jesus Christ is the kingdom of God and the way to reach it. The first step on this journey to the kingdom of God is to repent, which should be done from a broken Spirit and a broken and contrite heart through the Word and the Holy Spirit, and it should be proved by the deeds.

Luke 9:23, Matthew 10:28

"If anyone would come after me, he must deny himself and take up his cross daily."

Mark 10:39, Matthew 20:23

"You will drink the cup I drink and be baptized with the baptism I am baptized with."

Romans 6:3,4 Philippians 3:10-11, Colossians 2:11-12, 3:5

The true repentance makes it possible for His followers to participate in His sufferings and also share His Glory, the kingdom of God, through resurrection. The Way is on Horizon.

Isaiah 35:8-10

"And a highway will be there; it will be called the Way of Holiness. The unclean will not journey on it, it will be for those who walk in that way. But only the redemption of the Lord will walk there and the ransomed of the Lord will return. They will enter Zion with singing; everlasting joy will crown their heads and sorrow and sighing will flee away."

This Scripture foretold well the way. The redeemed and the ransomed of the Lord have become holy in Jesus Christ because Jesus

Christ became for us wisdom from God; our righteousness, holiness, and redemption (1 Corinthians 1:30). They are to journey along the Way of Holiness.

Acts 1:3
"After His suffering He showed himself to these men and gave many convincing proofs that He was alive. He appeared to these men over a period of forty days and spoke about the kingdom of God. His teaching from the beginning to the end is the kingdom of God through resurrection."

John 14:4
"Jesus Himself is the way and also the way to the kingdom of God."

Chapter 9

⸙

THE ROADMAP (NAVIGATION) TO THE KINGDOM OF GOD.

Sanctification

John 17:17
"Sanctify them by the truth; your Word is truth."

Through sanctification, man realizes that the body is the means by which the Holy Spirit works so that the body may be transformed by the Word and by participating in the baptism of death of Jesus Christ, becoming like Him, becoming like God in true righteousness and Holiness (quoted Philippians 3:10-11 and Ephesians 4:24) which leads to resurrection, eternal life, adoption as children of God, and the redemption of bodies.

"Burying with Jesus Christ into the baptism of death" is to burn away all impurities and all idols which come from man's sinful nature. The power of God from the Word, along with the work of the Holy Spirit, transforms the believer to be like Jesus Christ and God in true righteousness and holiness, taking off the old self of the worst sinner and putting on the new self; that is, sanctification to the redemption of the body, to become children of God.

The Kingdom of God

Genesis 3:23-24
"So the Lord God banished him from the Garden of Eden to work ground from which he had been taken. After he drove the man out, He placed on the east side of the Garden of Eden cherubim and flaming swords flashing back and forth to guard the way of the tree of life."

Matthew 3:2-3
" 'Repent, for the Kingdom of heaven is near.' This is he who was spoken of through the Prophetof through the Prophet Isaiah"…

Matthew 4:17
"From that time on Jesus began to preach, 'Repent, for the Kingdom of heaven is near.'"

Luke 4:43
"I must preach the kingdom of God to other towns also, because that is why I was sent."

According to God's salvation plan foretold in Isaiah, God sent Jesus Christ in order to recover the lost Kingdom of God to man, where he can again eat of the tree of life, which is the Word, giving back eternal life to man. Right after Satan's temptation in the desert, Jesus Christ proclaimed: "Repent," which is a mandatory condition to receive back the Kingdom of God as John the Baptist did. Jesus made it clear the reason why God had sent Him, in Luke 4:43 and also in Luke 19:10.

1 John 3:8

"He who does what it sinful is of the devil, because the devil has been sinning from the beginning. The reason the Son of God appeared was to destroy the devil's work."

Luke 17:21

"…because the kingdom of God is within you."

In the kingdom of God, the Word and the Holy Spirit work together fully according to the will of God.

Matthew 12:28

"But if I drive out demons by the Spirit of God, then the kingdom of God has come upon you."

God's salvation plan to recover the kingdom of God to man is to destroy the work of Satan by the Word, Himself and the Spirit of God (the Holy Spirit) so that they may be set free from Satan's temptation. Faith from the Word is for the born- again for resurrection for the kingdom of God by sharing in Jesus's sufferings, becoming like Him in His death through the Word and the Holy Spirit, through which man attains to the kingdom of God.

He concluded His earthly life right before departing from His disciples by convincing them that He was resurrected and spoke about the kingdom of God over a period of forty days right before His ascending. (Acts 1:3)

Jesus Christ was born for the kingdom of God, and preached the kingdom of God, and died for the kingdom of God for the lost people of God, to restore the kingdom of God to them.

The Road to the Kingdom of God

Being united with Jesus Christ in His death and also with His resurrection, taking off the old self and putting on new self, through faith in the power of God who raised Jesus Christ from the dead, with the power of the Word and the Holy Spirit for the hope of resurrection in Jesus Christ, becoming like God in true righteousness and Holiness, and then as Jesus said in Luke 17: 21 "The Kingdom of God is within you."

Related Scriptures:
John 5:3-5; Colossians 1:5, 23; Romans 6:2-7; 10:9-10, 10:17; Colossians 2:11; Romans 8:23-24, 8:9-14; Philippians 3:10-12; Ephesians 4:24

Today
"Thus far has the Lord helped us." (Isaiah 17:12)

Matthew 3:2-3
"…and saying, 'repent, for the kingdom of heaven is near. This is he who was spoken of through the Prophet Isaiah: A voice of one calling in the desert, prepare the way for the Lord, makes straight paths for him.'"

Psalms 2:7, Acts 13:33
"I will proclaim the decree of the Lord: He said to me you are my Son; today I have become your Father. He has fulfilled for us, their children, by raising Jesus. As it is written in the second psalm: 'You are my Son; today I have become your Father.'"

God, the Father who sent Jesus Christ, said, "Today I have become your Father" when He was raised for us by the power of the Spirit of God. (Romans 1:4) Jesus' teaching of the resurrection and the kingdom of God is in present and present perfect tense. "If anyone would come after me, he must deny himself and take up his cross daily and follow me."Luke 9:23

It can be illustrated in this way: If anyone wants to enter the Kingdom of God, today he must be born again, by taking up his cross every day with the Word and through the Holy Spirit. The concept of the entire New Testament for man's salvation is for today; neither for yesterday nor for tomorrow. For "yesterday" slipped away and is no more ours, and "tomorrow" is uncertain. You may cease your breath overnight, or you may be tempted, and fall by Satan, or Jesus Christ may return before the dawn of tomorrow. God did not say "Tomorrow you will be my Son," or "Tomorrow I will be your Father."

Hebrews 3:13
"But encourage one another daily, as long as it is called today, so that none of you may be hardened by sins' deceitfulness."

Hebrews 3:15
"Today if you hear His voice, do not harden your heart as you did in rebellion."

2 Corinthians 6:2
"In the time of my favor I heard you and in the time of salvation I helped you. I tell you, now is the time of God's favor, and now is the day of salvation."

John 8:11

"Jesus said to the woman to be stoned to death because of her act of adultery, 'Then neither I condemn you.' Jesus declared, 'Go now and leave your life of sin.'"

Today, now, leave your life of sin; you must put to death all the idolatries coming from your sinful nature: sexual immorality, lust, greed, and evil desires. Even the worst sinner is forgiven today, only if he repents with a broken and contrite heart and proves his repentance in everyday living.

1 Samuel 7:12
"Thus far, has the Lord helped us."

God has given us eternal life; the life is in His Son. (1 John 5:11)

Today when you hear His voice, and the Spirit of God knocks on your mind and heart and awakes your spirit (soul),

Today repent and turn to God and prove your repentance by your everyday living.

Today be transformed.

Today be born again.

Today be resurrected in Jesus Christ.

Today be created like God in true righteousness and holiness.

Today be the children of God.

Today receive the kingdom of God.

There will be neither the opportunity to be born again nor the kingdom of God through resurrection forever for you, unless you have them in this present world.

Today

"Finished and resurrected by the Spirit of God, who had been in Jesus Christ all the way of from the Virgin Mary's conception of him to the death on the Cross and his dead body, as today he became the Son of God, Christ, our Lord." (Hebrews 5:5, Romans 1:4)

Today if the Spirit of God who raised Him from the dead lives in us, God who raised Jesus Christ from the dead will give us new life through His Spirit who lives in us. (Psalms 2:7, Romans 1:4, 8-11, Acts 13:33)

Today God becomes our Father and we are sons and daughters of God through His grace. Jesus came to the earth to show man how to be children of God by His resurrection in Him. (Romans 8:13-14)

Today is not to be missed.

Forty Years

Deuteronomy 8:2
"Remember how the Lord your God led you all the way in the desert these forty years, to humble you and to test you in order to know what is in your heart whether or not you would keep His commands."

Deuteronomy 8:3
"He humbled you, causing you to hunger and then feeding you with manna, which neither you nor your forefathers had known, to teach you that man does not live bread alone but on every word that comes from the mouth of the Lord."

Deuteronomy 8:1
"Be careful to follow every command I am giving you today, so that

you may live and increase and may enter and possess the land that the Lord promised on Oath to your forefathers."

A man's life is divided, in general, into three chapters:
Birth to 20 years old—preparing for life
20 to 60 years old—active life
60 years to death—retiring from active life

The forty years covering 20-60 years old is a period that man is to eat manna, the Word in maturity according to God's salvation plan, and he must come to realize that the way to the kingdom of God is not by the visible materials of this world but every Word that comes from the mouth of God, because the kingdom of God is not of the world. (John 18:36)

The Son of God, who is greater than Moses, says, "Repent, the kingdom of God is near," and also "The kingdom of God is within you."

The forty central years of a man's life is the period during which man is to be born again for the resurrection in Jesus Christ for the kingdom of God through the Word and guidance of the Holy Spirit from God, the Father, the Gracious, the Almighty, for which Jesus came to this world. (Luke 4:43)

Jesus Christ, right before starting to preach the kingdom of God, showed the way, through Matthew 4:4-10, to the kingdom of God at His temptation, subsequent to forty days' fasting in the desert, of Satan and the test of God. "Manna" is the Word, the revelation of God, through the Son of God in the New Testament. The Promised Land is the kingdom of God in the New Testament.

The Hope in the Gospel

The hope in the gospel is integrated (interrelated) with resurrection, eternal life, the adoption as the children of God, and the redemption of bodies and the Kingdom of God.

Matthew 4:17

"From that time on Jesus began to preach, 'Repent, for the kingdom of heaven is near.'"

Jesus' public ministry after the temptation in the desert was inaugurated by His announcing that to have a hope for the coming kingdom of God means leaving the past life of sins. This is necessary to have a hope of eternal life, which "God, who does not lie, promised before beginning of time." (Titus 1:2)

1 Peter 1:3

"In His great mercy, He has given us new birth into and living hope through the resurrection of Jesus Christ from the dead."

A living hope for the kingdom of God through the resurrection of Jesus Christ reflects what Jesus said in John 3:3-5, implying that Jesus Christ is Himself the kingdom of God, and Paul's saying in Romans 6:5-6 that "If we have been united with Him in His death, we will certainly be united with Him in his resurrection. For we know our old self was crucified with Him so that the body of sin might be done away with."

Romans 15:19

"If only for this life we have hope in Christ, we are to be pitied more than all men."

Luke 17:21

"Because the kingdom of God is within you."

Titus 1:2

"A faith and knowledge resting on the hope of eternal life…"

1 Peter 1:4

"… and into an inheritance that can never perish, spoil, or fade, kept in heaven for you."

As you will note in the above four verses, the hope in the gospel is concerned with both the present world as well as that which is to come.

-Question: Where is the hope?
-Answer: The hope is in the gospel of God's grace.

Colossians 1:23

"If you continue in your faith established and firm, not moved from the hope held out in the gospel."

What is the hope held out in the gospel?

Ephesians 4:24

"…and to put the new self, created to be like God in true righteousness and holiness…"

The true righteousness and holiness in God give birth to the eternal life into the kingdom of God.

How do we get the true righteousness and holiness? They are in Jesus Christ who has become for us wisdom from God – that is our righteousness, holiness, and redemption. (1 Corinthians 1:30)

1 John 5:11

"And this is the testimony: God has given us eternal life, and this life is in His Son."

1 Corinthians 1:30

It is because of Him (God) that you are in Christ Jesus, who has become for us wisdom from God. That is our righteousness, holiness, and redemption. Jesus Christ Himself is the resurrection, eternal life, and the Lord of the kingdom of God through whom we have eternal life into the kingdom of God.

Romans 8:23-24

"As we wait eagerly for adoption as sons, the redemption of our bodies. (Which is our resurrection in Jesus Christ.) For in this hope we were saved."

Romans 8:25

"But if we hope for what we do not yet have, we wait for it patiently."

Isaiah 40:31

"But those who have hope in the Lord will renew their strength. They will soar on the wings like eagles; they will run and not grow weary, they will work and not be faint."

Romans 15:13

"May the God of hope fill you with all joy and peace as you trust in Him so that you may overflow with hope by the power of the Holy Spirit."

Colossians 1:23
"This is the Hope from the Gospel..."

The hope is that God, who saves even the worst sinner of the sinners through the Son and the Holy Spirit, will recreate us in His true righteousness and Holiness into the redemption of body for eternal life in the Kingdom of God.

In this hope, we are always joyful and give thanks to God in all circumstances.

Implications of the Tests and Temptations of Job and Jesus Christ

There are two great happenings in the history of the Bible.
-The test of Job, who was God's faithful servant but only full human. (Job 1:8-13)
-The test and temptation of Jesus Christ, who was full human but also full divine. (Matthew 1-3)
-Both were performed by Satan under the supervision of God.
-Job was God's faithful servant who trusted God so much that God allowed Satan
to test him.
-Job had great faith; under such unbearable and miserable situations, having been stripped of all he had except his life, as God ordered to Satan, he never cursed God.
-I know that my redemption lives, and that in the end he will stand upon the earth. And my skin has been destroyed, yet in my flesh I will seek God.
I myself see him with my own eyes—I, and not another. (Job 19:25-27)

- Against his wife's last offense, "Are you still holding to your integrity? Curse God and die," he replied, "Shall we accept good from God and not troubles?" (Job 2:9)

- His vindication toward God. He asked why God was turning His face from him, trying to convince Him that there was no reason for God to be so unjust to him.

The Lord's answer came to Job out of a storm: "Who is this that darkens my counsel with the words without knowledge?" (Job 38:2)

His answer was not only to Job and his friends but also more to Satan, implying that God would send the living Word of truth, the Son that God will allow Satan to tempt so that Satan should realize what is "the Word with knowledge," which would crush Satan. As said in Matthew 4:4, "Man does not live on bread alone, but on every Word that comes from the mouth of God," setting His lost people free from the power of Satan. The Word with which Jesus Christ frustrated Satan's temptation has been working among His believers to recover the Kingdom of God to them.

What matters in the two tests is "with the Word without knowledge and with the Word with knowledge."

The Greatest of These Is Love

1 Corinthians 13:1-3
"Love is patient, love is kind. It does not envy, it does not boast, it is not proud. It is not rude, it is not self-seeking, it is not easily angered, it keeps no record of wrongs. Love does not delight in evil but rejoices with the truth. It always protects, always trusts, always hopes, always perseveres.
And now these remain; faith, hope, and love. But the greatest of these is love."

Love described in these verses is a virtue of the believers, whether they are Christian, Buddhist, Confucian, so on. It was also the main teaching of sages like Mencius or Lao-za, in the East, with some different wording but the same meaning.

But the love of Christians should be pursued not from the men's teaching requiring man's efforts of self-discipline or self-culture, which have intrinsic limits due to man's sinful nature.

There are a couple of scriptures of Paul's contradicting "the greatest is love."

Colossians 1:5

"…the faith and love that springs from hope that is stored up for you in heaven—the gospel has come to you."

Colossians 1:23

"…if you continue in your faith, established and firm, not moved from the hope held out in the gospel, this is the gospel that you heard and has been proclaimed—and of which I, Paul, have become a servant."

Paul has become a servant for the gospel of the steadfast faith not moved from the hope in the promise of God from the gospel, and he would stand on trial because of his hope in resurrection of the dead. (Acts 23:6)

For Christians, the love in these verses of 1 Corinthians 13:3-7 is a byproduct which comes from new creation by faith in Jesus Christ, for faith is to express itself through love for born-again Christians born of the Spirit of which the first fruit is love, joy peace, patience, kindness, goodness, faithfulness, gentleness and self-control. (Galatians 5:6 and 5:22)

Love, for Christians, is to share with the world the good news of resurrection for the kingdom that comes through faith and hope.

Why did Paul declare to the Corinthians "the greatest of these is love"?

Nobody would doubt that Paul's faith and hope for adoption as sons, the redemption of the body which is resurrection, for which he risked his life, might have faded, when he wrote the book of Corinthians.

The clue should be found in unique surroundings faced by the early Christians of Corinth in its cultural and life settings. Corinth was heavily influenced by Greek philosophy and its immorality, including religious prostitution; what was worse, there was bitterness from fractions and divisions, divided by followers of Paul, Apolos, Cephas, and Christ, in which Jesus Christ was considered to be one of the teachers. In this infant stage of the Corinthian church, Paul must have focused on preventing any breakage of the church by taking the verses of love as the greatest first aid.

Even though the love of self-discipline and self-culture has an intrinsic limit due to man's sinful nature, Paul must have judged that it would serve to heal the bitterness and bind up divisions and fractions which were caused by such hazardous cultural and life settings.

Therefore, the verses should be interpreted in the light of particular cultural and life settings.

"The greatest of these is love for you, Corinthians, in your present situation."

The Truth of Salvation

The fall of man was due to man's inherent fat portions (sinful nature) which are vulnerable to all kinds of temptation by Satan.

Whether they were inhabited by Satan or they belonged to parts of

God's salvation plan is not clearly known. According to Leviticus 3:16, all fats are the Lord's, and they must be burnt away, which means they are not of Satan.

In the New Testament it was also mentioned: "Those who belong to Jesus Christ have crucified the sinful nature" (Galatians 5:24) and they have to be put to death. (Colossians 3:5, 2:11)

When God asked the first man "Where are you now?" in Genesis 6:9, God should have meant "Do not run away to hide yourself from the sin you had committed, giving poor excuses, but now repent what you have done wrong, because you are in my hands wherever you try to hide yourself."

God's grace to man is: Now, today, repent, turn to God and prove your repentance by living, forgetting what is behind and straining toward what is ahead as Paul said in Philippians 3:13, before it is too late. For there is neither resurrection nor the kingdom of God for eternal life unless you attain them through the Word and the Holy Spirit while living in this world now, today, when you are favored by His grace.

Jesus declared the truth of God's salvation for man in the Words of truth of God in John 8:11. "Then neither do I condemn you. Go now and leave your life of sin."

This is God's verdict to the woman who was supposed to be stoned to death because of her adultery.

Christianity

To the Christian, the cross is a departing station from death to life, from the part of sinful nature to "born again" new life of today toward the resurrection which is to happen while living in this world.

The resurrection through being born again and sanctification is to happen now because Jesus said "the kingdom of God is within you." Luke 17:21

Repenting the sinful past, turning to God and proving repentance by today's life creates new life, where there is no more sinful past but only today's new life, which proceeds toward the kingdom of God.

"Blessed are they whose transgressions are forgiven, whose sins are covered."

"Blessed is the man whose sin the Lord never counts against him." (Romans 4:7)

"Go now and leave your life of sin." (Matthew 8:11)

Today, believers should purchase a ticket for the journey along the route of being born again and resurrection in Jesus Christ to the kingdom of God. The ticket is free of charge, not from anything of this world, but with the Word and the Holy Spirit, which is the grace of God.

The ticket of only accepting the work of the Word and the Holy Spirit must be kept with the faith through the grace of God, until reaching and passing the gate of the kingdom of God, which will stretch from today to the eternity.

The resurrection is to be attained "through the fellowship of sharing in His sufferings, becoming like Him in His death" (Philippians 3:10-11), having been buried with Him in baptism and raised with Him through your faith in the power of God, who raised Jesus Christ from the dead (Colossians 2:12) and putting on a new self, created to be like God in true righteousness and holiness (Ephesians 4:24).

Unless the resurrection is attained today while we are living in this world, there is no more resurrection, which is the graceful gift of God to His lost peoples, once for all to us, because today is the departing station for the resurrection to the kingdom of God for Christians. There is no more sinful past but only today's resurrection through being born again toward the Kingdom of God as long as the ticket is not lost, as Paul said in Philippians 13:13. "Forgetting what is behind and straining toward what is ahead."

When Jesus said "I tell you the truth" in the gospel, He was telling the truth of God is to happen now in present tense for tomorrow where there is no more sinful past:
"Today you are my Son."
"Today I am your Father."

The longest human life, a little over a hundred years from birth to the tomb, is nothing but the instrument (furnace) through which new birth is to be attained by the power of the Word and the fire of the Holy Spirit with the hope for resurrection in Jesus Christ toward the kingdom of God, eternity.

Christianity is today's life for today's resurrection toward the Kingdom of God, which is the yoke and the load for the Christians to take up in this world.

Christians have both privilege and accountability to share this blessing with the world.

"To do good work" as mentioned in the gospel is condensed into sharing this good news of God's grace with the world, by living as a stranger in this world.

Yoke and Load

Man's life is like a journey under a yoke and a load; the yoke is on his neck and the load is on his back. What the yoke and load to take is a crossroads for life to eternity or to destruction. To believers, it presents very significant implications in setting steps toward the kingdom of God, whether for present life or the one to come through resurrection in Jesus Christ.

The yoke of Jesus Christ:

-The sacrifice of atonement for man's sin to God.

—Resurrection to be the Son of God and become Christ, Messiah. (Romans 1:4, Acts 2:36)

-Showing to believers the way to the kingdom of God and spreading the good news of the kingdom of God in the whole world to all nations. (Matthew 4:17, 4:23; Luke 17:21; Matthew 28:18; Acts 4:8; Luke 24:47-49; Matthew 9:35; Luke 11:20; Matthew 12:28; Matthew10:38; Matthew 16:24; Mark 8:34; Luke 9:23; Luke 14:27, Mt20:23, Mis10:39)

The load of Jesus Christ:

-Being crucified on the Cross for the sacrifice of atonement for man's sin, which also shows the Way to the believers to be born again.

-Extensive training of the twelve apostles to become His witnesses to the whole world.

The Yoke of Paul and the Apostles

-Witnessing, testifying, and proclaiming Jesus from birth, through His life, suffering, resurrection, and ascension, as well as sharing His teachings. (Acts 1:8, Acts 17:18, Acts 4: 33, Acts 23:6, Acts 23:11, Acts 1:22; Luke 24:45-49; Matthew 28:18)

-Making Jesus' disciples in the whole world to all nations, which is the great mission from Jesus Christ. (Matthew 28:18)

The Load of Paul and the Apostles

-Setting up the churches for home bases to advance their yoke.

-Risking their lives to the death of crucifixion in the steps of Jesus Christ, having been accompanied by severe persecution and sufferings beyond description. (2 Corinthians 1:8-9; 2 Corinthians 11:24-28; Galatians 6:17; Philippians 3:8

The Yoke of the Believers

-Establishing the kingdom of God within them (Luke 17:21) through born-again resurrection in Jesus Christ by sharing Jesus' suffering, becoming like Him in His death (Philippians 3:10, 6: 3-6), and thus recovering true righteousness and holiness to be like God (Ephesians 4:24), and entering the Kingdom of God. (John 3:5; Romans 6:3-5, Romans 8:23, Romans 12:1; 1 Peter 1:3; Romans 6:5; Philippians 3:11; Ephesians 4:24; Hebrews 12:14; 1 Peter 1:15-16

The Loads of the Believers

-Confessing that Jesus is the Lord, the Son of God by believing that God raised Him from the dead, resurrected in the heavenly body, which is the perfect resurrection.

-Being forgiven of sins by grace of God through faith in the work of the Word and the Holy Spirit through repentance of a broken spirit and a broken and contrite heart by being buried with Jesus Christ in His baptism of death, taking off the old self and putting on the new self.

-Living out the new life through faith in the freedom according to guidance of the Holy Spirit, in which the believers taste the kingdom of God on the earth.

-Becoming true disciples and sharing in proclaiming the great mission of Matthew 28:18; to outside churches as well as inside. (Matthew 20:22, 23; Mark 10:39; 1 John 1:25, 27; John 1:41; Matthew 16:16; Romans 6:3-5, Philippians 3:10; Ephesians 4:22; Hebrews 12:4; Colossians 2:5; Romans 8:23-25; Romans 12:1-2; Hebrews 10:5; Matthew 1:20, Luke 1:35)

The Yoke is the Way God purposes man to pursue all along in the life-long journey toward the destination. The Load is the baggage to carry on their back until the Yoke on their neck is completed to the destination. The gospel encourages believers to live this world as "strangers" to carry and finish the Yoke and Load as God purposes.

Headship of Man and Woman

In the light of new covenant of Jesus Christ and the Holy Spirit, the title is to be reviewed, which will stand in contrast to Genesis chapter 1 and the other scriptures related.

Jesus said, "I am telling you the truth" in the gospel. He meant that he was telling you in the place of God, not as a man a born of the Virgin Mary, but as of the God conceived of the Holy Spirit.

John 11:27
" 'Yes, Lord,' she told him, 'I believe that you are the Christ, the Son of God, who was to come into the world.' Jesus made the woman Martha to confess the great faith which has been handed down to this day."

John 4:21-35
Jesus was teaching the Samaritan woman the essence of the gospel:
-Where to worship God
-How to worship him
-Salvation coming to any believer, not only a Jew—whoever believes, and worships Him in the Spirit and truth.
-The Samaritan woman was despised and the adulterous woman had five husbands.

But Jesus made the woman His servant, the first evangelist to proclaim Him as Christ to her fellow Samaritans: "I who speak to you am he." (John 4:26)

Jesus said to the disciples who complained of Jesus contacting the Samaritan woman, "My food is to do the will of Him who sent me and finish His work—open your eyes and look at the fields, they are ripe for harvest." Jesus knew the woman's potential power as a believer of faith, being capable of evangelism.

Matthew 28:10
"Then Jesus said to them [Mary Magdalen and the other Mary], 'Do not be afraid. Go and tell my brothers to go to Galilee; there they will see me.'"

Jesus made the women who followed Him, at the risk of their lives, the first servants to proclaim His resurrection, ahead of His disciples.

Acts 2:17-18
The new covenant of the Holy Spirit: "In the last days, God says I will pour out my spirit on all your people. Your sons and daughters will prophesy. —- Even on my servants, both men and women.

Romans 12:6-8
We have different gifts, according to the grace given us.

The leadership in today's world, whether in the church or Christian families, setting apart the non-Christian world, should be harmonious, according to the gifts given by the grace of God.

Matthew 9:17
"No, new wine into new wine skins, and both are preserved."

"The Truth Will Set You Free"

John 8:31
"If you hold to my teaching, you are really my disciples. Then you will know the truth, and the truth will set you free."

How does the truth set man free? And where is it from?

The truth is from the Word, which is Jesus Christ, who has become for us wisdom from God that sets man free by establishing our righteousness and holiness and redemption (quoted from 1 Corinthians 1:30) in the believer.

In the Old Testament, in Peter 9:10, the fear of the Lord is the beginning of wisdom. In the New Testament, 2 Peter 2:22 related with wisdom:

"A dog returns to its vomit, and a sow that is washed goes back to her wallowing into the mud."

Those who do not have wisdom of the truth from the Word and who go back to commit sins, criminal acts, bad habits, and all kinds of follies along with faults are compared to animals.

Therefore, the truth of the Word, who is Jesus Christ, sets the believer free from such animal-like behavior, through the wisdom from God. That is righteousness, holiness, and redemption.

"Man of Little Faith"
John the Baptist

Luke 7:28
"I tell you, among those born of woman, there is no one greater than John;
yet he who is least in the Kingdom of God is greater than he."

John 1:33
John the Baptist gave this testimony: "I saw the Spirit come down from heaven as a dove and remains on him. The man on whom you see the spirit comes is he who will baptize you with the Spirit."

John 1:34

"I have seen Him and testify that this is the Son of God."

John 1:29

"Look, the lamb of God, who take away sin of the world!"

Those scriptures are the great testimony of John the Baptist about Jesus Christ.

Luke 7:19-20

"Are you the one who was to come, or should we expect someone else?"

Contrary to his great testimony, John the Baptist was still skeptical about Jesus Christ. Jesus' main teaching is the kingdom of God through resurrection that originates from the faith in Jesus Christ.

Jesus said to Thomas, "You saw and believed but blessed are those who have not seen but believed." The kingdom of God has been mostly for those who have not seen but believed in Him.

But John the Baptist saw Him and made a great testimony about Him, and yet his suspicion was lingering, as a man of little faith. Those who have not seen Him but believed in Him by faith are by far greater than John the Baptist. Jesus' saying "he who is least in the kingdom of God is greater than he" means John the Baptist is a man of little faith, considering that the kingdom of God is for those who have faith in Jesus Christ.

Therefore, John the Baptist may be the greatest born of woman on the earth, but he is lesser then he who is least in the kingdom of God. John the Baptist baptized with water, but he did not have a chance to be baptized with the Holy Spirit and live by faith that comes from the Word. For the Kingdom of God is for those who do not see Jesus Christ but believe in Him by faith from the Word.

Stream of Living Water

John 7:37-39

"If anyone is thirsty, let him come to me and drink."

Whoever believes in Him, as the Scriptures said, a stream of living water flows from within him. By this He meant the Spirit, which those who believed in Him were to receive.

Jesus said in John 6:63, "The Spirit gives life; the Words I have spoken to you are spirit and they are life."

He also said in John 6:54, "Whoever eats my flesh and drinks my blood has eternal life."

The "stream of living water" has already been in Jesus through the Word which is His flesh and blood. Therefore the "stream of living water" flows within Him from the time whoever believes in Jesus Christ in true righteousness and holiness. The Holy Spirit, the Counselor, helps the believer to have the stream of living water flow from within him with steadfastness.

The Book of Esther
(No Name of God)

The name of God was not mentioned at all in this book. "If I perish, I perish." was desperate cry facing the most imminent and grave situation under which the name of God is to be called. No matter what reason lies underneath, it is regarded as God's intention. Instead of calling the name of God, the book is characterized by fasting in sackcloth with the cry, "If I perish, I perish."

Fasting helps to empty one's mind and body, making the person denying himself and humble for the cause he fasts for, by indwelling the Holy Spirit so that God works in His way in the person, which is also the intention of fasting, to show his determination toward God.

Wearing sackcloth was and is still now the eastern tradition during the period of mourning for the death of the nearest family members as well as national disaster.

This book teaches to call the name of God in a humble, earnest, and contrite attitude, from the heart.

"I live in a high and holy place but also with him who is contrite and lowly in spirit." (Isaiah 57: 15)

"This is the one I esteem: He who is humble and contrite in spirit and trembles at my word." (Isaiah 66:2)

God gives a significant message in this book not to call Him habitually, not in vain, but in such an earnest attitude so that He may be attentive. The attitude of fasting in sackcloth with a cry of "If I perish, I perish" is equivalent to calling God by His name from the attitude of the humble, earnest, and contrite heart.

Salt

Matthew 5:13
"You are the salt of the earth. But if the salt loses its saltiness, how can it be made salty again?"

Colossians 4:6
"Let your conversation be always full of grace, seasoned with salt, so that you may know how to answer everyone."

"Seasoned with salt"—having been baptized with graceful fire of the Word and the Holy Spirit, and being led by them, then you may know to answer everyone in the way God wants you to speak to the world. If you lose the power of the Word because of your selfish interests from your sinful nature, longing for the present world, you will become like the salt which has lost its saltiness, only to be dumped away.

Division and Peace in Luke 12:49-51

"I have come to bring fire on the earth, and how I wish it were kindled! But I have baptism to undergo, and distressed I am until it is completed. Do you think I came to bring peace on earth? No, I tell you, but division."

Mark 10:39
"Jesus said, 'You will drink the cup I drink and be baptized with the baptism I am baptized.'"

Mark 3:11 (Luke 3:16)
"He will baptize you with the Holy Spirit and fire."

-Baptism: to undergo Jesus' crucifixion on the Cross for the atonement for men's sin, and for the believers' putting off the old self and putting on the new self.
-Fire: the power of burning away man's fat portion which is the sinful nature by the Word and the Holy Spirit.
-The faith in the power of God who raised Jesus Christ from the death separates the believers creating division from this world, which is division made by fire of baptism through the Holy Spirit.

John 14:27
"Peace I leave with you; my peace I give you. I do not give you as the world gives."

-The peace Jesus mentioned in Luke 12:51 is a worldly peace, which is to be broken easily due to man's sinful nature at the temptation of Satan as well as evil powers of this world. The peace Jesus gives is real peace, which can't be broken away because the fire of Jesus' baptism has been kindled and spreading as the believers participate in his baptism of death, which creates holiness in righteousness free from sinful nature to be like men of God.

"But the mind controlled by the Spirit is life and peace." (Romans 8:6)

-Fellowship with God in His holiness and true righteousness by faith in Jesus Christ brings forth real peace, which comes from the kingdom of God, which has already been established in you.

Contemporary Interpretation of the Jerusalem Council

Acts 15:29
"You are to abstain from food sacrificed to idols, from blood, from the meat of strangled animals and from sexual immorality."

-Idols are all things that belong to earthly natures: sexual immorality, impurity, lust, evil desires, and greed, which is idolatry. Colossians 3:5

-You are not to desire anything that comes from these idols and also not to be infected or influenced or contaminated by the people who are engrossed (involved) in these idols.

-You are to keep away from any practice to exploit anyone by choking for selfish interest for the purpose of material gains, which is strangling the man God created in His image. Those who do it are bloodsuckers. Those who are choked will experience dying, loss of life.

Their grief at losing life will reach God.

God's retribution will be imminent.

-Sexual immorality will bring about the breakage of the principal order of social structure of which a unit is family, which will eventually cause a more horrible disaster than nuclear bomb or a volcano eruption: a breakage of social structure.

"No free will" is the only way to the kingdom of God.

2 Corinthians 1:18-20

"But as surely as God is faithful, our message to you is no 'yes' and 'no.'

For the Son of God, Jesus Christ, who was preached among you by me, Sila, and Timothy was not 'yes and no' but in me it has always been 'yes' in Christ.

For no matter how many promises God has made, they are 'yes' in Christ."

-The Old Testament is considered the context of God's command to His people regarding obedience or disobedience, which alludes to "free will" given to the first man, while the New Testament is the story of one way to God's grace (the Word and the Holy Spirit through Jesus Christ) for man's salvation, which is the only way to reach the Kingdom of God.

Once the grace of God has come, by indwelling among us, "free will to choose "yes or no" is invalid. Only "yes" toward God's grace is the teaching of the gospel of the New Testament to enter the kingdom of God.

Romans 6:3

"Or don't you know that all of us were baptized into Jesus Christ were baptized with Him through baptism into death, in order that just as Jesus Christ was raised from the dead through the Glory of the Father, we too may have a new life."

-By burying not only our sinful nature with its practices, but also the whole body into the death of Jesus Christ through the Holy Spirit by faith in Him, man will have new life through the Spirit of God, as also said in 1 Peter 2:5, "Offering spiritual sacrifice acceptable to God through Jesus Christ."

Hebrews 10:15 (Psalms 40:6)

"Sacrifice an offering you did not desire, but a body you prepared for me;

with burnt offering and sin's offering you were not pleased."

"No free will" through the grace of God makes it possible for the believers, by faith, to participate in Jesus' suffering and death, putting off the old self, putting on a new self, and becoming like Him in his death, somehow attaining to resurrection, created to be like God in His righteousness and holiness. (Philippians 3:10-11, Ephesians 4:24)

The grace of God, which is the Son (the Living Word) and the Holy Spirit transformed "free will" in the Old Testament into "no free will" in the New Testament, completing both the Old Testament and the New Testament into one, which is totally integral will of God for the salvation of man, freeing His lost people from the power of Satan.

"The free will" given to the first man is only a shadow of God's plan to change it into "no free will" through His salvation plan.

"No free will" is the only way for believers to be the children of God and see Him and to enter the kingdom of God through the resurrection in Jesus Christ.

The Son of God offered Himself as a whole burnt offering, a sacrifice of an atonement for man to God—how much more the sinful man is to offer the whole soul, mind, and body as a living sacrifices, not conforming any longer to the pattern of this world, holy and pleasing, acceptable to God (Romans 12:1), which is "no free will" to the kingdom of God.

One way with "no free will" to the kingdom of God: faith through the Word—participating in Jesus' sufferings and death—being born again as children of God through the Holy Spirit—resurrection in Jesus Christ.

The kingdom of God of today in you will be kept eternally through this one way of no free will.

The Forfeited Soul for This World

Matthew 16:26
"What good will it be for a man if he gains the whole world, yet forfeits his soul? Or what can a man give in exchange for his soul?"

Psalms 49:7-9
"No man can redeem the life of another or give to God a ransom for him –the ransom for a life is costly, no payment is ever enough—that he should live on forever and to see no decay."
-How and why does he forfeit his soul?

He loves this momentary world so much as to sell his soul to sin from the sinful nature (fat portion) which belongs to this earthly nature: sexual immorality, impurity, lust, evil desires, and greed, which is idolatry (Colossians 3:5), as if this world would last forever.

Neither anyone nor anything on the earth can redeem the mortal to be immortal. The Son of God, who was raised from the dead by the

Spirit of God, can redeem him who has faith (from the Word) in Jesus' sacrificial atonement for man's sin.

"Whoever eats my flesh and drinks my blood will have eternal life." identifies with taking the Word in the Spirit so that the Word may become the flesh and the blood.

"For you have been born again, not of perishable seed, but of imperishable through the living and enduring Word of God" (1 Peter 1:23), repenting from the contrite heart, turning to God, and proving repentance by living.

Matthew 8:5
"Blessed are the pure in heart for they will see God."

Who are the pure in heart?

Colossians 3:5
"Put to death, therefore, whatever belongs to your earthly nature: sexual immorality, impurity, lust, evil desires and greed, which is idolatry."

The eyes are the lamp of the heart. The pure in heart have good eyes because their hearts are freed from the idolatry which blinds the eyes to God.
Therefore, the pure in heart have good eyes to see God, who promises that they will inherit the kingdom of God.

Matthew 16:17-23 regarding
"You are the Christ, the Son of the living God."

16:17"Blessed are you, Simon son of Jonah, for this was not revealed to you by men, but my Father in heaven."

16:18"And I tell you that you are Peter, and on this rock I will build my church…"

16:19"I will give you the keys of the kingdom of heaven; whatever you bind on earth will be bound in heaven, and whenever you loose on earth will be loosed in heaven."

16:23 "Get behind me Satan! You are a stumbling block to me; you do not have in mind the things of God, but the things of Satan."

"On this rock I will build my church":

The son of Jonah, Simon's confession, "You are the Christ, the Son of the living God" is the testimony of the truth, the rock, which points to Jesus Christ, on which the church is to be built.

The testimony of truth was revealed by God, not any man, nor Simon. The church can never be built on the man's name of Peter, only son of Jonah who is nothing but human, having disowned Jesus three times contrary to his assertion against which Jesus said to Peter, "Get behind me, Satan! You are a stumbling block to me. You do not have the things of God, but the things of men."

Any church which has not been built on the truth "Jesus is the Christ and the Son of the living God," not with the things of God but with the things of man, is to be involved with grave feud, whether Catholic or Protestant.

The church built with the things of man is to be tumbled down as Peter disowned Jesus Christ at the mercy of Satan.

-The Key for the Israelites

Acts 2:36
"Therefore let all Israelites be assured of this; God has made this Jesus whom you crucified, both Lord and Christ."

Acts 2:38

"Repent and be baptized, every one of you, in the name of Jesus Christ for the forgiveness of your sins. And you will receive the gifts of the Holy Spirit."

The gift of the Spirit is leading the believer to the kingdom of God through faith in the truth.

This is the first key given to Peter for Israelites.

-The Key for the gentiles

Acts 10:28

"He said to them, 'You are well aware that it is against our law for a Jew to associate a gentile or visit him. God has shown me that I should not call any man impure or unclean. So when I was sent for, I came without raising any objection.'"

Acts 2:34-35

"Then Peter began to speak: 'I now realize how true it is that God does not show favoritism, but accept men from every nation who fear Him and do what is right.'"

"Do what is right," according to the truth that Jesus is the Christ and the Son of the living God and His teaching. The testimony of the truth "Jesus is the Christ and the Son of the living God" in order to become as a member of God's family, whether Jew or gentile, is the key to the kingdom of God. This is the key for the gentiles given to Peter. Whatever you bind on earth will be bound in heaven, and whatever you loose on earth will be loosed in heaven.

Whenever you bind or loose on earth in making the family of God (Ephesians 2:16-17) toward the kingdom of God based on the testimony of the truth, it will be also accepted in heaven.

Matthew 28:18-20

"All authority in heaven and on earth has been given to me, therefore go and make disciples of all nations, baptizing them in the name of the Father and of the Son
and of the Holy Spirit, and teaching them to obey everything I have commanded you. And surely I am with you always, to the very end of the age."

-Forgiving sins by fixing the stamp of God's ownership on the believers as children of God, liberating them from the slaves of Satan is the crown of authority of all other authorities. (Mark 2:7) Who can forgive sins but God alone?

-Baptizing in the name of the Father and the Son and the Holy Spirit cleanses all sins, all impurities, and all idols through being born again, for the resurrection in Jesus Christ, to the kingdom of God through the Trinity: God, the Father, the planner of salvation for man through the Son, and the Holy Spirit; God, the Son, the Messiah for forgiveness of man's sins through his blood on the Cross to recover the kingdom of God to his believers; and God, the Holy Spirit, the permanent counselor for the redemption of the body, resurrection in Jesus Christ as children of God

-"Teaching what I have commanded you"—His main teaching is the kingdom of God, which comes from being born again: resurrection in Jesus Christ through faith in sharing in His baptism of death and the power of God who raised Jesus Christ from the dead. (Matthew 4:17, John 3:3-5, Acts1:3-4) The greatest commandment is "Love the Lord, your God with all your heart and with all your soul and with all your mind," (Matthew 22:37) and the second is "love your neighbor as yourself." (Matthew 22:39)

-"And surely I am with you."

"The virgin will be with child and will give birth to a son, and they will call him Immanuel, which means "God with us."

God is with us not only at the present but to the very end the age as said, "the Word became flesh and made His dwelling among us." (John 1:14)
"Man does not live on bread alone, but every Word that comes from the mouth of God." (Matthew 4:4)

Jesus Christ is in us with His Word, forever and ever.

What is "believing in Jesus Christ?"

-    It is believing in His mysterious birth:
Full divine being conceived of the Holy Spirit
Full human being born of the Virgin Mary

-The Son of God, Jesus Christ our Lord
full divine by His resurrection. (Romans 1:4)

-His teachings:
Mathew 4:17
"Repent, for the kingdom of God is near."
John 3:3
"No one can see the kingdom of God unless he is born again."
John 3:6
"No one can enter the kingdom of God unless he is born of water and the Spirit."
Acts1:3
"After His suffering, He showed himself to these men and gave many convincing proofs that He was alive. He appeared to them over a period of forty days and spoke about the kingdom of God."

-His resurrection and the kingdom of God is His main teaching from the beginning to the end, through being born again and resurrection and the believer's resurrection in Him.

The kingdom of God through being born again involves forgiveness of sins from tearful repentance and the baptism of washing away sins, sharing in His sufferings, becoming like Him in His death, taking off the old self and putting on the new self, which is a new creation.

-His Ascension

-His second coming to judge the living and the dead.

The Kingdom of God Revealed in Matthew 4:4-10 and 6:24

Matthew 4:1
"Man does not live on bread alone, but on every Word that comes from the mouth of God."

The kingdom of God is not a matter of eating and drinking, but of righteousness, peace, and joy in the Holy Spirit. (Romans 14:17)

Righteousness, peace, and joy in the Holy Spirit are produced by the Word inspired by the Spirit of God, which is the revelation of God Himself.
Therefore, in order to be in the kingdom of God, the believer is to take up his cross every day, being seasoned himself with the Word of God and the Holy Spirit.

Matthew 4:7
"Do not put the Lord your God to the test."

As Peter 3:5-6 says, "Trust in the Lord with all your heart and lean not on your understanding; in all your ways acknowledge Him." This clarifies that the believer is to be entirely devoted to God, the Father almighty, without any speck of suspicion.

Matthew 4:10
"Worship the Lord your God, and serve Him only."

Deuteronomy 6:4: "The Lord is One. Love your God with all your heart and all your soul and all your strength." This is declared as the first commandment, that the believer cannot serve both God and Mammon (anything from man's sinful nature) in the kingdom of God. You cannot serve two masters in the Kingdom of God.

"From that time on Jesus began to preach the kingdom of God," (Matthew 4:17) until He stayed with His disciples for forty days after His resurrection, right before His ascension.

Jesus' experience of temptation by Satan in the desert is understood as pre-showing his main teaching on the earth how the kingdom of God is established either in this world or in that which is to come, and also is God's testing of Jesus Christ regarding how to establish the kingdom of God in Jesus Himself before He preaches it to men.

Resurrection and the kingdom of God in the believer are to be measured by the standard of God, because there is no one righteous in the eyes of God.

The Hope in the Gospel

The hope in the gospel is integrated (interrelated) with resurrection, eternal life, the adoption as the sons of God, and the redemption of bodies.

Matthew 4:17

"From that time on Jesus began to preach, 'Repent, for the kingdom of heaven is near.'" Jesus' public ministry after the temptation in the desert was inaugurated. announcing to have a hope for the coming Kingdom of God leaving the past life of sins, to have a hope of eternal life, which "God, who does not lie, promised before beginning of time." (Titus 1:2)

1 Peter 1:3

In His great mercy, He has given us new birth into and living hope through the resurrection of Jesus Christ from the dead. A living hope for the kingdom of God through the resurrection of Jesus Christ reflects Jesus' statement in John 3:3-5 implying that Jesus Christ is himself the kingdom of God, and Paul's saying in Romans 6:5-6, "If we have been united with Him in His death, we will certainly be united with Him in his resurrection. For we know our old self was crucified with Him so that the body of sin might be done away with."

Romans 15:19

"If only for this life we have hope in Christ, we are to be pitied more than all men."

Luke 17:21

"…because the kingdom of God is within you."

Titus 1:2

"A faith and knowledge resting on the hope of eternal life."

1 Peter 1:4

"…and into an inheritance that can never perish, spoil or fade—kept in heaven for you."

As we notice in the above four verses, the hope in the gospel is concerned with both the present world as well as that to come.

-Question: where is the hope?
-Answer: the hope is in the gospel.

Colossians 1:23
"If you continue in your faith established and firm, not moved from the hope held out in the gospel."

What is the hope held out in the gospel?

Ephesians 4:24
"…and to put the new self, created to be like God in true righteousness and holiness."

The true righteousness and holiness in God give birth to eternal life in the Kingdom of God. How do we get true righteousness and holiness?

1 John 5:11
"And this is the testimony: God has given us eternal life, and this life is in His Son."

1 Corinthians 1:30
"It is because of Him (God) that you are in Christ Jesus, who has become for us wisdom from God. That is our righteousness, holiness, and redemption."

The wisdom from God shows the way to the kingdom of God through Jesus Christ.

Romans 8:23-24

"…as we wait eagerly for adoption as sons, the redemption of our bodies, which is our resurrection in Jesus Christ, for in this hope we were saved."

Romans 8:25

"But if we hope for what we do not yet have, we wait for it patiently."

Isaiah 40:31

"…but those who have hope in the Lord will renew their strength. They will soar on the wings like eagles. They will run and not grow weary, they will walk and not be faint."

Romans 15:13

"May the God of hope fill you with all joy and peace as the trust in Him so that you may overflow with the hope by the power of the Holy Spirit."

The hope is that God who saves even the worst sinner of the sinners through the Word and the Holy Spirit will recreate us in His true righteousness and holiness into the redemption of body for eternity. In this hope, we're always joyful and give thanks to God in all circumstances. This is the hope in the gospel.

The Word – God Breathed

John 6:53

"I tell you the truth, unless you eat the flesh of the Son of Man, and drink His blood, you will have no life."

Eating and drinking symbolize believing in He who calls the believers to drink the cup He drinks and be baptized with baptism He is baptized with (Mark 10:38-39), which enables them to experience His sufferings by faith in the Word, putting off the old self and putting on the new self. For Jesus Christ who is the living Word gives life, supplying a spring of living water which is the fountain of life.

Therefore, eating and drinking is to take the Word and its Spirit by faith so that they may indwell among the believers, which gives eternal life. Related scriptures:

John 6:63
"The spirit gives life; the Words I have spoken to you are spirit and they are life."

John 7:38
"Whoever believes in me, as the Scripture has said, streams of living water will flow within him."

John 6:35
"I am the bread of life. He who comes to me will never go hungry, and he who believes in me will never go thirsty."

John 6:68-69
"You have the Words of eternal life. We believe and know that you are the Holy One of God."

John 8:51
"Anyone who keeps my Word will never see death."

1 John 5:11-12

"God has given us eternal life, and this life is in His Son. He who has the Son has life."

John 1:14
"The Word become the flesh and made His dwelling among us."

How and what do we become to acknowledge from the Bible?

Because all Scripture is God-breathed (2 Timothy 3:16), one should read it in the spirit, repeatedly, with prayers in spirit also, not influenced by anything from this world or by our sinful nature.

The Holy Spirit will guide the reader to realize that the Bible was written either by the inspiration of God or the revelations of God, which gives the faith not moved from the hope established and firm which is held out through the gospel:

-God, the Father Almighty—planner of salvation for man

-God, the Son—Messiah by His resurrection

-God, the Holy Spirit—the permanent counselors with the believers

-Incarnation of Jesus Christ, full divine and full human

-Jesus' sacrifice of atonement for human beings' sin

-Jesus' resurrection and the believers' in Him toward the kingdom of God through the Holy Spirit

-Jesus' ascension

-Jesus' second coming

Chapter 10

A Layman's Fragments of Faith

"Circumcision in the Heart by the Spirit"
Competed on the Cross of Jesus Christ

Galatians 5:6
"For in Jesus Christ neither circumcision nor uncircumcision has any value. The only thing that counts is the faith expressing itself through love."

Galatians 16:15
"Neither circumcision nor uncircumcision means anything; what counts is new creation."

Did Paul deny the circumcision?

Genesis17:11
"You are to undergo circumcision, and it will be sign of covenant between me and you."

The covenant:

Genesis17:14 "I will be your God."

Genesis 17:9 "You will keep my covenant."

Genesis 22:8 "Abraham answered, 'God Himself will provide the lamb for the burnt offering, my son.'"

Romans 4:11

"And he received the sign of circumcision, a seal of righteousness that he had by faith."

-Paul points out that the covenant was initiated by God to the righteousness by Abraham's faith. "God himself will provide the lamb for burnt offerings or God has the power to raise the dead to life."

Paul's challenge to circumcision is the sign of circumcision (covenant) vs. a seal of righteousness.

The former is outward; the latter is inward.

Deuteronomy 10:16

"Circumcise your hearts, therefore, do not be stiff-necked any longer."

Deuteronomy 30:6

"The Lord your God will circumcise your hearts and the hearts of your descendants, so that you may love Him with all your heart in all your soul and live."

Leviticus 26:40-41

"But if they will confess sins and the sins of their fathers—their treachery against me, which made me hostile toward them so that I sent them into the land of their enemies—then when uncircumcised hearts are humbled and they pay for their sins."

Genesis 9:26

"For all these nations are really uncircumcised, and even the whole house of Israel is uncircumcised."

Romans 2:29

"No, a man is a Jew if he is one inwardly; circumcision is circumcision of heart by the Spirit, not by written code."

As God saw Israelites who had the sign of covenant of circumcision committing sins and treacheries against Him, He sent them to the lands of enemy so that they realized their sins and confessed, and the written codes could not circumcise their hearts.

"The circumcision in the heart by the Spirit" is on the horizon. Here are the dialogues between God and the Son:

Psalms 2:7-8

"I will proclaim the Decree of the Lord; He said to me, 'You are my Son; today I have become your Father.'"

Psalms 40:6-8

"Sacrifices and offering you did not desire but my ears you have pierced; burnt offerings and sin offerings you did not require. Then I said, 'Here I am, I have come—it is written about me in the scroll, I desire to do your will, O my God. Your law is written in my heart."

-The scriptures signify that God was executing His salvation plan for man by sending the Son to solve the problem which the written codes could not.

John the Baptist testified that the one on whom the Holy Spirit comes down would baptize with the Holy Spirit and fire.

Romans 8:3

"For what the law was powerless to do in that it was weakened by the sinful nature, God did by sending His own Son in the likeness of sinful man to be a sin offering."

Acts 7:51

"You stiff-necked peoples with uncircumcised hearts and ears. You are just like your fathers: you always resist the Holy Spirit! I have baptism to undergo. "

Romans 6:3-4

"Don't you know all of us who were baptized in Jesus Christ were baptized into His death."

John 3:5

"I tell you the truth, no one can enter the kingdom of God unless he is born of water and the Holy Spirit."

The Kingdom of God is to be established through being born again, by participating in Jesus' baptism of death on the Cross by faith through the Holy Spirit in the power of God who raised Jesus Christ from the dead. Unless you are born again by participating in Jesus' baptism of death through the Holy Spirit by faith in the power of God who raised Jesus Christ from the dead, and become children of God, you can't enter the Kingdom of God, in which the circumcision in the heart by the Spirit has been completed.

Galatians 6:14

"May I never boast except in the Cross of our Lord, Jesus Christ, through which the world has been crucified to me, and I to the world."

Therefore in Jesus Christ neither circumcision nor uncircumcision has any value.

"The only thing that counts is expressing itself in love." (Galatians 5:6) "What counts is new creation." (Galatians 6:15)

Both verses clearly declare that change must happen inwardly as well as outwardly; there must be total circumcision as well as total baptism.

Colossians 2:11
"In Him you were also circumcised, in putting off the sinful nature, not with a circumcision done by the hands of men but with a circumcision done by Christ, having been buried with Him in baptism and raised with Him through your faith in the Power of God, who raised Him from the dead."

-The circumcision, which still remains as one of the main teachings of Judaism, is no longer a valid relic of the Old Testament to modern Christians, but it has to be considered to have been completed by the baptism of death of Jesus Christ on the Cross into the spiritual baptism to the modern believers according to God's gracious salvation plan for man.

Abraham's faith in God gave birth to circumcision; the sign of covenant believers' faith in the Power of God who raised Jesus Christ from the death gave birth to the spiritual baptism, the seed of righteousness. The same faith toward the same God is one of the main pillars supporting both the Old Testament and the New Testament respectively, as circumcision in the Old Testament and baptism in the New Testament play their roles in the entire Bible.

Luke 12:10

"And everyone who speaks a word against the Son of man will be forgiven, but anyone who blasphemed against the Holy Spirit will not be forgiven."

There are two titles that Jesus called Himself: the Son of God and the Son of Man. The Son of God was conceived of the Holy Spirit; the Son of Man was born of the Virgin Mary. Everyone against the Son of Man can be forgiven by the grace of God. But anyone against the Holy Spirit will not be forgiven because the Holy Spirit is God himself. Therefore, everyone against the Son of God who was conceived of the Holy Spirit and his miracles will not be forgiven either, because the miracles were performed of the Spirit.

A Layman's
Fragments of Faith

-God, the Creator cannot be crucified.

God is the Spirit. (John 4:24)

God, as the Creator, cannot be crucified either by Satan or any of his creatures, because of the Spirit.

The Spirit who was in the dead body of Jesus Christ born of the Virgin Mary made Him alive to be resurrected as the perfect Son of God, who has become wisdom for us from God that is our righteousness, holiness, and redemption (1 Corinthians 30), which is God's plan for man's salvation to destroy Satan and burn away man's sinful nature with the power of the Word and through the fire of the Spirit through Jesus Christ, who was chosen before the creation of the world, and has become the Son of God, our Lord by His resurrection.

- In the gospel, when Jesus said, "I tell you the truth," He meant, "What I say is the truth from God. I am speaking as God on behalf of Him; God the Father, the Son, and the Holy Spirit of the truth." The Word is truth of God.

- Either the Word or prayer not in the Spirit has no power that comes from God.

- Jesus' blood shed on the Cross is the blood which has overcome all man's sin, which was shed on behalf of man. It has power to cleanse the believer's sin only if he accepts it through faith in the power of God, who raised Jesus Christ from the dead.

- The Trinity may be represented by the work of truth, holiness, and righteousness.

- Jesus' saying "take up your Cross daily and follow me" (Luke 9:23) is the principle of "Today" which encompasses the past, present, and future, which are one in God.

Today, be born again and resurrected to receive the Kingdom of God.

Psalms 2:7 "Today I have become your Father."

Psalms 95:7 "Today if you hear His voice..."

Hebrews 3:15 "Today, if you his hear His voice..."

- The Gospel is the good news of man's salvation from God that man is justified by faith in Christ, the Son for hope to be resurrected in Christ who is the Word

-The power of small mustard seeds:

- The Kingdom of God; Jesus Christ who was born in a manger and worked only as a carpenter has impacted the world far beyond human imagination, establishing the Kingdom of God in believers.

- One phrase of His teaching has transformed the world as well as the worst sinner incredibly.

- Jesus trained twelve disciples who were from the grass roots, and who with no education became the apostles and the witnesses of the gospel to the whole world.

- Faith in resurrection of Jesus Christ who was raised from the dead by God, in hope for our resurrection in Him for the kingdom of God, eternal life, which is the Word of faith to be proclaimed to the world.

- Jesus Christ has completed the road map to the Kingdom of God in such a short period.

- Christian life should be shaped as described in 1 Thessalonians 5:16 "Be joyful always."
We should be joyful because we hope to be adopted as the children of God, for the kingdom of God.
"Pray continuously."
Because praying is communication with the living God that all things should be done according to His will by the spirit indwelling among us.
"Give thanks to God in all circumstances."

Because we trust that God works good for those who love Him and have been called according to His purpose, and from Him, through Him, to Him are all things.

- Predestination in Ephesians 1:5 and Romans 8:28

God, the Creator predestined His salvation plan to save His lost people from the power of Satan through the Word without fail; the lost sheep recognize the shepherd's voice which is the Word of God, through Jesus Christ. (John 8:47, 10-27)

- Dying in Christ is to create new life by sharing His sufferings in His believers, which is to be born again for resurrection in Him.
- Christ's blood works for the forgiveness of sins and the redemption of the body only when his Spirit indwells among the believers. (Ephesians1:7; Romans 8:9-10)
- The gospel calls the believer to be born again by the baptism of the Spirit through faith from the Word, and to be filled with Holy Spirit for the redemption of the body to be adopted as children of God, which is the resurrection for the kingdom of God.
- Colossians 1:5 and 23 discuss faith from the hope for resurrection in Jesus Christ.
- Jesus Christ had to undergo the baptism of death on the Cross to be the Christ, thus opening a new world for the believers, which is the Kingdom of God. He was born and died to give the kingdom of God to the believer. He proclaimed it from the beginning and addressed the resurrection for the kingdom of God to the disciples right before his ascension to God, who had sent Him for this purpose.
- The work of the Trinity for man's salvation from Romans 8:10-14:
Verse 10 - the work of Christ
Verse 11-13 - the work of God
Verse 14 - the work of the Holy Spirit (see also Titus 3:5-7)

- Sanctification produces fruits of the Spirit (Galatians 5:22) because sanctification is the work of God through the Word and the Holy Spirit. Through the Word by the Spirit, believers put to death the misdeeds of darkness and the sinful nature with its practices, which belong their earthly nature.
- Nobody with man's sinful nature can enter the Kingdom of God, regardless of whether he is the greatest, the richest, etc. unless he is

born again, resurrected in righteousness and holiness. Even of the Son of Man who was born of the Virgin Mary took off the human body on the Cross, because God is Holy and His dwelling place is also holy. Jesus Christ showed the way to the kingdom of God.

- Predestination

God's salvation plan for man is predestination through the Word, through which all people lost to Satan are to be saved back without fail. The sheep recognize the shepherd's voice. (John 10:27) The sheep listen to His voice, the Word. (John 8:47)

- The believer's life is an ongoing war against the idolatries of the sinful nature, which are the baits of Satan.
- Those who triumph over spiritual warfare are to gain physical redemption, which is resurrection in Jesus Christ.
- Jesus' crucifixion on the Cross denotes Christ as sacrificial atonement to God for man's sin, and also the way for man to become children of God taking off the sinful old self and putting on a new self in Him.
- Even the Son of Man returned to God, the Father by doing so to become to be the Son of God; how much more are sinful men to become the children of God?
-Jesus' resurrection through the Spirit of God three days after His death has opened a new way to worship God: worshiping Him in spirit and truth. (John 4:23
Not on the Sabbath but on the Lord's day newly established through Jesus' resurrection.
Not in the temple of the synagogues, but in the churches
Not proclaiming the Law and the prophets but Jesus Christ as the Lord, the Son of God, who gives the kingdom of God through resurrection in Him.
All these should be, as Jesus Christ said, "new wine in new wine skins," which is the New Testament.

- Those who trust in God with all their spirit will be empowered by the Holy Spirit.

- Jesus Christ's proclaiming the Kingdom of God after His painstaking experience as a human to build earthly houses as a carpenter 2000 years ago implies the greater hardship involved in building the Spiritual kingdom of God. As said in Acts 14:22, "We must go through many hardships to enter the kingdom of God."

Faith - Love – Hope

1 Thessalonians 1:2 & Colossians 1:5

Faith expresses itself in love, which prompts labor and thus produces the work of faith, which requires endurance, being inspired by hope of being "born again," the redemption of bodies, children of God, and the Kingdom of God.

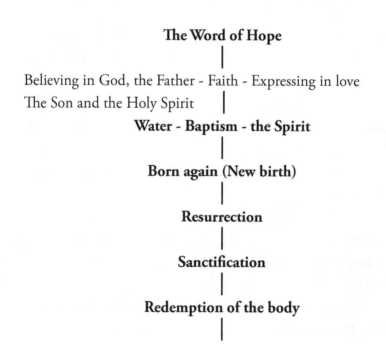

The Son   - God -   the Holy Spirit

The Word of Hope
|

Believing in God, the Father - Faith - Expressing in love
The Son and the Holy Spirit |

Water - Baptism - the Spirit
|

Born again (New birth)
|

Resurrection
|

Sanctification
|

Redemption of the body
|

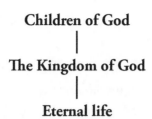

Children of God

|

The Kingdom of God

|

Eternal life
The grace of God revealed in John 17:17-19 and 14:16-17;
His salvation plan for man.

After many agonies, such as bleeding, as the Son of Man, the baptism of sufferings on the Cross (Luke 4:42 and 44), Jesus confirms why He was sent to the earth by God, the Father, and manifested His determination like His will to the disciples as well as the believers by acknowledging God's salvation plan for man to be sanctified on the Cross on behalf of His lost peoples so that they may be sanctified not on the cross, but by the Word that is the truth as described in James 1:18, John 1:14, Romans 6:3-4, Colossians 2:11-12, 1 Peter 1:23-24, John 6:54.

He promised to send another counselor to be with us forever in order to complete God's salvation plan, as evidenced in Romans 8:11, 13-14; Titus 3:5-7.

The symbols of materialism in the New Testament

- Matthew 26:15
Thirty visible silver coins were more valuable than the invisible kingdom of God in his teacher whom he served as a master.

- Matthew16:26, Luke 11:20
What will it be good for a man if he gains the whole world, yet forfeits his soul? Or what can a man give in exchange for soul?

The symbols of nonmaterialism in the New Testament

- Mark 10:21

"Go, sell everything you have and give to the poor, and you will have treasure in heaven. Then come, follow me."

- Mark 5:13

With the sacrifice of 2000 pigs, one man bound with evil spirits was saved by Jesus. How much value did 2000 pigs have in those days?

- Matthew 13:44

"...for the Kingdom of God, selling all he had."

- Hebrews 10:5-6

"Sacrifice and offering you did not desire, but a body you prepared for me.

With burnt offerings and sin offerings you were not pleased."

Wisdom

1 Corinthians 1:30

"Who has become for us wisdom from God."

This is:

Our righteousness through faith from the Word (John 8:5) and Our holiness through the baptism of death (Romans 6: 3-4, Philippians 3:10) and our redemption of the body through being born again/resurrection (John 3:3-5, Philippians 3:11) and through sanctification (Romans 8:14, John 17:17 & 19), which is through the Word and the Holy Spirit.

The righteousness, holiness, and the redemption are prerequisites to enter the kingdom of God. Jesus Christ, who has become wisdom from God for us, is the wisdom for us to enter the kingdom of God.

Jesus Christ was sent by God to give us the wisdom to enter the kingdom of God, which Jesus Christ proclaimed from the beginning to the end. The faith in resurrection of Jesus Christ who was raised by God, the Father, and in hope for our resurrection in Him for the kingdom of God, eternal life through Jesus Christ, the Son of God is the Word of faith that should be proclaimed to the world.

- Growth in faith transforms the believer and sanctifies him toward resurrection for the kingdom of God.

-Those who trust in God with all their hearts and spirits will be empowered by the Holy Spirit.

- John 8:51

"I tell you the truth, if anyone keeps my Word, he will never see death."

When Jesus said, "Repent, the kingdom of God is near," he brings the kingdom of God through the Word, which is Himself; the resurrection and the eternal life. As He said, "The Words I have spoken to you are the Spirit, and they are life. (John 6:65)

- Without sufferings in Jesus Christ, there is no being born again, no resurrection, no kingdom of God, either present or the future, no children of God, no eternal life.

"I tell you the truth"

"I" means the Word, which is the truth. The Word is God. (John 1:1) Jesus Christ is telling the truth of God, which makes new creations in Jesus Christ, transforming the old into the new, which is born again toward resurrection in Jesus Christ through the Holy Spirit for the kingdom of God to eternal life.

The truth of God.

The truth of the Son.

The truth of the Spirit.

God is the truth, so is the Word.

This is the truth Jesus Christ declares as a new covenant to His believers. "I will put my law in their minds and write it on their hearts. I will be their God and they will be my people. No longer will a man teach his neighbor, or a man to his brother, saying 'know the Lord,' because they will all know me, from the least of them to the greatest.

For I will forgive their wickedness and will remember their sins no more." (Jeremiah 31:33-34)

- The gospel is the good news for man's salvation from God that man is justified by faith in Jesus Christ, who is the Word, the Incarnate, for hope to be resurrected in Christ through the Holy Spirit which leads to the kingdom of God, eternity.

The treasure of the gospel in its nature is too valuable to be kept in any kind jar of clay and is to be transferred according to the freedom of the Spirit as it works for the salvation plan of God.

- Christians' yoke and load is to share the treasure of salvation from the gospel until time matures according to the planner's timetable.

- With the pain of childbirth in order to be born again in putting off old self with its sinful nature, there should be children born of God; because God is holy, He asks believers to be holy to be accepted as His children.

-Without being led by the Word and the Holy Spirit, there will be no children of God, no Kingdom of God, and no eternity.

Romans 10:8-10

That is the Word of faith we are proclaiming; that if you confess. We are not proclaiming the Word of love, because faith is expressing itself through love. (Galatians 5:6)

Our faith is in Jesus' crucifixion on the Cross, through which, as Paul said, "the world was crucified to me and I to the world" (Galatians 6:14). This creates new creation through the Spirit of God. (Romans 8:11)

Therefore what counts is a new creation through salvation in Jesus Christ, as Paul said in 2 Corinthians 5:17 & 19

Therefore if anyone is in Jesus Christ, he is a new creation.

The old one has gone!

The new one has come!

The new creation does not count man's sins against him.

This is the word of faith we are proclaiming to the world.

-The yoke on the neck

The yoke of sinful nature - death

The yoke of legalism - no salvation

The yoke of faith - eternity

-There is no room for the Holy Spirit and the Word to work even in believers these days:

- Excessive attachment to the idols and gods of this age.

- Being kept too busy, being occupied by the desperate need not to get behind the pattern of this world.

- Becoming the slaves to the production of modern technology rather than to the Word.

-Galatians 6:4-5

"Without comparing himself to somebody else, for each one should carry his own load."

What a wonderful person is he or she who does not compare

himself (herself) to somebody else and carry his own cross as he or she was created by the Creator, without grumbling, in Jesus Christ. Such a person can also share the cross (loads) of others.

- Dual meaning of Christ's suffering (sacrifice):

- Atonement for man's sin to God

- The way for the believer to turn to God

The baptism of Jesus was to undergo the baptism of fire (death) on the Cross on behalf of man's sin, that the baptism of fire may be flamed into the believers by faith through the Word and the Holy Spirit, which gives birth to being born again, a new creation to be the children of God, promising to His believers resurrection in Jesus Christ for the kingdom of God, for which He was born and died.

Unless everyone undergoes this baptism of death in this world, there will be no more being born again in the coming world.

God sent the Word and the Holy Spirit through Jesus Christ so that man's sinful nature would be burnt away as the fat portions on the altar had to be, because no one can hear the voice of God, nor see Him, nor so much as see the kingdom of God, nor enter it, unless they become holy by burning away the sinful nature (the fat portions).

-Circumcision in the Old Testament is completed in the New Testament as shown in Colossians 2:11-12. Both circumcision and baptism involve pain and suffering.

- Outwardly cutting off or putting off the old one to have a new mark on the body

- Inwardly turning to God by repentance from the contrite heart, crucifying the sinful nature (fat portions)

Baptism is to be followed by suffering, dying, burial, and resurrection in Jesus Christ. (Romans 2:4, Philippians 3:10-11, Colossians 2:11-12)

- Undergoing the baptism of the believer

By faith, sharing in Jesus' sufferings through the Holy Spirit, repenting with tears from a broken and contrite heart, turning to God and proving repentance by living.

- The believer's life is to be the war against the idolatries from the sinful nature caused by Satan's temptation.
-John 12:25

The man who loves his life will lose it, while the man who hates his life in this world keeps it for eternal life.

The man who lives his life in sinful nature, dealing with this world as if it would last forever without being born again, will lose his life even in this world, not so much as in the world to come.

He who hates the life of a sinful nature and wants to be transformed by the Word and the Holy Spirit will have new life, leading to eternity.
- God, in His plan to terminate Satan, had Satan choose to tempt or test the first man, Job, and Jesus Christ. God turned the tables to fulfill His plan in the world of His creatures. That is the mystery of God, which was purposed in Jesus Christ.
- Being born again with the Word and the Holy Spirit surely destroys the work of Satan, which drives out Satan from the believer.
- Eternity is for those who do not put attachment to anything in this world but make the most use of it to attain born-again status in the hope for resurrection toward the Kingdom of God, living like a stranger.
- Jesus was taking off His humanity on the Cross to return to God, thus

setting the way for us to do the same. "What counts is new creation." (Galatians 6:14)

- Man's life from the first cry at birth to the last breath is to be like a furnace in which new birth is to be molded through the grace of God: the Word and the Holy Spirit.

- When human sinful nature is enticed by Satan's temptation, God may use it for His discipline, testing, or punishment, because God disciplines those He loves, and punishes everyone whom He adopts as His children. (Hebrews 12:6)

- The fullness of both the Word and the Holy Spirit is the stage of the believer's resurrection in Jesus Christ for the Kingdom of God.

- The Lord who was conceived of the Holy Spirit cannot be crucified, because He is God. God is the Spirit. The Spirit cannot be crucified. Jesus who was born of the Virgin Mary was crucified, "who had been chosen before the Creation of the world, but was revealed in there last times for your sake." (1 Peter 1:20)

- Jesus who is coming again is not full divine and full human, but just full divine.

- Jesus Christ, who is the image of God, is born of the Virgin Mary; so was the first man, Adam. (Genesis 1:26)

-Jesus Christ who is exact representation of His being (Hebrews 1:3) is born of the Holy Spirit.

- The mystery

God's salvation plan through Jesus Christ with the Word and the Holy Spirit to terminate Satan among His creatures is the mystery from God.

1 Corinthians1:29-30

Jesus Christ has become for us wisdom from God—that is, our righteousness, holiness, and redemption:

without righteousness there is no reconciliation with God.

without holiness there is no way to see God.

without redemption there is no way to the kingdom of God.

The wisdom of righteousness, holiness, and redemption makes it possible to set believers free from those evil desires and behaviors of effrontery, brazen impudence, a beast with human face, and man's face but brutes in mind (the beast's mind).

- God is the God for those who pursue, by faith, being born again—resurrection in Jesus Christ for the kingdom of God in the midst of struggling against sin, and yet do not follow the phantom (pattern) of this world, but who are transformed by the grace of God: the Word and the Holy Spirit.

- Christianity should be reflected in life itself, taking up the cross every day in Jesus Christ.

- Faith should be everyday actual living, because faith is to express itself in love. (Galatians 5:6)

- The book of John can be titled the book of "I tell you the truth." The Word is the truth, the truth of God, the Father, the Son, and the Holy Spirit. Jesus Christ is the truth, Himself. He declared the truth in terms of "who I am" and "what I am."

- The seed of the Word is fully grown to faith; sharing in Jesus' sufferings in baptism of death through faith in the Power of God who raised Jesus Christ from the dead gives birth to being born again and resurrection in Jesus Christ for the kingdom of God.

- The entire fourteen books of Paul's Epistles are summed up as describing the way to the believers' resurrection in Jesus Christ, as He was by the Power of the Spirit of God, through which man (the believer) enters the kingdom of God. (2 Corinthians 12:2-4)

- Eternal life is not a goal to achieve but grace to be received by faith in Jesus Christ through the Word and the Holy Spirit.

- Do not make any idol from excessive gratefulness toward man, and do not make any idol from hatred against man, for all things are from, through, and to Him, God.

- Unfinished grace is also His total grace through which God completes His purpose.

- Being a good citizen in the world is only one of the preconditions to be a good citizen in the kingdom of God, for being born again is mandatory to enter the Kingdom of God.

- Live by the Spirit and the Word, lest one should be turned over to the unmerciful trampling of Satan.

- Predestination through the Word

God's salvation plan for man is that through the Word, through which all His lost people are to be saved back from Satan without fail, the sheep recognize the shepherd's voice and listen to His voice. (John 8:47 and 10:27)

Without the Word there is no faith, no being born again, no resurrection, no children of God, no kingdom of God, and no eternity. The Word is the greatest favor to man from God, the greatest grace of God.

- Jesus Christ, who was resurrected, is not "full human and full divine" any longer, but He is full divine.

- How to interpret the happenings between God and Satan in Job 1:6-12

God made a pre-declaration of His plan to terminate Satan by sending the living Word, Jesus Christ, to destroy the impudence of Satan.

-Fruit of the Word - faith
-Fruit of faith - baptism with water and the Spirit
-Fruit of baptism – being born again
-Fruit of being born again – being adopted as children of God, redemption of the body, resurrection in Jesus Christ, the kingdom of God to

eternity through sanctification of the Word and the Holy Spirit.

- Unless a man is born again and resurrected in Jesus Christ who was crucified on the Cross for this purpose, which is the believer's ultimate hope toward the kingdom of God, faith and love will be vain. (Colossians 1:5, 1:23, 2:11-12 and Romans 1:17)
- "Born again" tells us "No" to ungodliness, "No" to the pattern of this world and its passions, living up to what he has gained through being born again by being upright, self-controlled in godly life, looking forward to the blessed hope of being adopted as a child of God, and redemption of the body, which is the resurrection in Jesus Christ toward the kingdom of God.

- Free will

There is no free will from God since He sent the Word, Jesus Christ, and the Holy Spirit.

There is only one way through the Word and the Holy Spirit to reach the destination of the eternal life to the kingdom of God. For free will is from man's sinful nature, which is vulnerable to Satan's temptation, which should be fired and burnt away by the Word and the Holy Spirit.

- Both the Word and the Holy Spirit have the power of fire to burn away all the idolatries from man's sinful nature, for the Word and the Holy Spirit is the Spirit of God.
- The baptism is to cross over the bridge of sin and death. "Born again with water and the Spirit" means to be baptized with the Word and the Holy Spirit, because repenting with tears from the contrite heart comes through the work of the Word and the Holy Spirit, which gives new life to cross over the bridge of sin and death.
- New birth by the Word

John 1:14

John 1:18

John 8:51

1 Peter 1:23-25

- New birth by the Holy Spirit

John 3:3-5

Romans 8:11, 14

Titus 3:5

- New birth by the Word and the Spirit

John 6:53

Jesus' body is the Word.

Jesus' blood is the Spirit.

-Jesus reconfirmed what He said in Luke 22:19-20. "This is my new covenant in my blood. This is my body, which is for you."

We must be committed to totally following Him through the baptism of fire with the Word and the Holy Spirit.

- Jesus' crucifixion on the Cross denotes Jesus' sacrificial atonement to God for man and also connotes the way for man to become children of God by taking off the old self and putting on the new self.

John 6:53-54

"I tell you the truth, unless you eat the flesh of the Son of Man, and drink His blood, you will have no life."

Eating and drinking means believing in Him who calls the believers to drink the cup He drinks and be baptized with baptism he is baptized with (Mark 10: 38-39) which is to enable them to experience His sufferings by faith in the Word, putting off the old self and putting on the new self. For Jesus Christ, who is the living Word, gives life, supplies the spring of living water, the fountain of life:

"The words I have spoken to you are spirit and they give life." (John 6:63)

Therefore, eating and drinking is to take the Word and the Spirit by faith so that he may dwell among the believers, which gives eternal life.

Related scriptures:

John 6:63, John 7:38, John 6:68-69, John 8:51, 1 John 5:11-12

God has given us eternal life, and this life is in His Son. He who has His Son has life.

God Cannot Be Crucified

God, the Creator, is the Spirit. As God, the Creator cannot be crucified, neither by Satan nor by any of his creatures. The Spirit who was in the dead body of Jesus Christ born of the Virgin Mary made Him alive to be resurrected as the perfect Son of God, who has become wisdom for us from God, that is our righteousness, holiness and redemption (1 Corinthians 1:30), which is God's plan for man's salvation to destroy Satan and to burn away man's sinful nature, the two obstacles against God's will (plan).

"Born Again"

Being born again tells us "No" to all kinds of idolatry, including sexual immorality, impurity, lust, greed, evil desires, etc. that come from man's sinful nature by living the life sanctified by the Word and the Holy Spirit, looking forward to the hope of being adopted as children of God, the redemption of the body, which is the resurrection in Jesus Christ toward the kingdom of God.

Purify your soul by putting to death those idolatries—sexual immorality, impurity, lust, greed, and evil desires—with the power of the Word and fire of the Holy Spirit as you do with your body by burning the fat of your body through everyday exercise.

- The cross for man to carry, which is the yoke on his neck and the load on his back as well as in the heart is to be borne every day, not for the sake of man's sinful nature but (for the sake of) righteousness, holiness, and redemption toward eternity en route to the present, and momentary, but long enough for His salvation plan for man.

- What does the faith from the gospel make possible?

Jesus Christ is the Lord, the Son of God, Messiah
Finite to infinite
Mortal to immortal
Visible to invisible
New Creation in Jesus Christ
All this is from God.

- Jesus Christ, as to human nature, was a descendant of David who was born of the Virgin Mary and became the Son of God by His resurrection, which took place through the power of the Holy Spirit. That also teaches mankind how to be children of God by resurrection in Him. (Romans 1:3-4, 8:11, 13-14)
- The punishment of disobedience which caused the fall of man due to the temptation of Satan, even if it was done through God's salvation plan to destroy Satan ,which is God's ultimate goal by sending the Son (the living Word) and the Holy Spirit, is not to be waived, according to God's righteousness, justice, and holiness, but is to be forgiven by the faith in Jesus Christ through God's salvation plan for man.

- Faith is the greatest response of man to God's grace, while the grace of God is the most supreme gift that man cannot imitate.
- One of the new words these days:
"Remake" instead of "being born again"
- Fire:
Choose the fire of the Word and the Holy Spirit to be born again, before the time set by God matures.

Man's Effrontery—Self-esteem

It is right that Jesus Christ died for our sin. But if we believe that the Spirit of whom Jesus was conceived also died, that is drastically wrong, because God is the Spirit, and Spirit in Jesus Christ is also God. (Matthew1:20, Luke 1:35)

Neither God nor the Spirit can be killed. (Matthew 10:28) God is only one who can kill both the body and the spirit. Man's notion that the Son of God died for our sin seems to come from man's effrontery—self-esteem and selfish comfort, which is also from man's sinful nature. The Son of Man who was born of the Virgin Mary was crucified. The Son of God who was conceived of the Holy Spirit was not crucified.

The Spirit in Jesus' dead body raised Him from the dead through the power of God as the completely resurrected body of the full divine.

Jesus's resurrected body is to show to man how man's body, dead to sin, is also to be raised as a resurrected body in Jesus Christ, if the Spirit of God lives in us, which is the grace of God for man's salvation.

Man's Oblivion

Psalms 40:5
"Many, O Lord my God, are the wonders you have done.
The things you planned for us.
No one can recount to you;
Were I to speak and tell of them.
They would be too many to declare.
I brought you out of Egypt, and took care of you in burning land.
When I fed you, you were satisfied,
When you were satisfied, you forgot."

Man is too forgetful.

Is this because modern-day people are too busy by being overwhelmed with so much, many things to do, including hanging on the computer, watching, playing, and talking on cell phones...? This may be partly true.

However, it has happened ever since the beginning, starting with the first man, who forgot God's command during a simple life in paradise, and the Israelites forgot God's command during their the simple life in the desert.

John 6:26
"I tell you the truth, you are looking for me, not because you saw miraculous signs but because you ate the loaves and had your fill."
Oblivion is inevitable because of man's sinful nature, vulnerable to Satan's temptation, which makes man inclined to give excessive value to the present need, forgetting more valuable things in the past as well as in the future to come. When we look back at the past of our life in faith, we will be amazed to find how God has worked uncountable wonders (miracles) in things small and large, and how He is also

working now in our present life. We shall be convinced that He will be also with us working for our future life to come.

Man's oblivion against God by Wonders of Grace will be under control through faith that comes from Power the Word and the Holy Spirit.

Man's disease of oblivion for the wonders of God's grace can be healed by the Word and the Holy Spirit.

By Faith
Hebrews 11:4-31

These scriptures listing the prominent men of faith in the Old Testament was titled a hall of fame for men of faith by someone who has a particular concern in faith.

Meanwhile, in the New Testament, by faith, Jesus Christ, who was born of the Virgin Mary took up the cross to be crucified for the atonement for man's sin and for being resurrected from the dead by the Spirit of God to become our Lord, Messiah, through which Jesus shows His believers how to be resurrected in Him.

By faith, the believers share in Jesus' sufferings, becoming like Him in His death and so, somehow, attaining to the Kingdom of God (Philippians 3:10-11), and by taking off the old self and putting on the new self, being created to be like God in His righteousness and holiness. (Ephesians 4:24)

The faith described in Hebrews 11:4-31 is only the beginning of faith to shape whole and complete one in Jesus Christ and His believers, through which God's salvation plan for man is to be completed.

The two greatest miracles Jesus Christ performed for God's salvation plan.

The first, being "born again" (John 3:2-6) is not by a second conception in woman's womb but by the Spirit, which opened the way to be the children of God, redemption of the body, and to the kingdom of God.

The second was that the twelve uneducated disciples were made apostles in such a short period that they were commissioned to undertake the great mission of Matthew 28:19 and Acts 1:8, which has established today's Christianity, building up the road to the kingdom of God through being born again to be the children of God, and redemption of the body, which is resurrection for the kingdom of God.

The first miracle is for the individual's new creation.
The second is for new creation from the individual to the world.

Excessiveness

1 Titus 6:10
"For the love of money is a root of all kinds of evil. Some people, eager for money, have wandered from the faith and pierced themselves with many griefs."

Any excessiveness from the sinful nature (seminal sins) of man destroys the room in the person in which the Word and Holy Spirit are to work to keep the creation of order for life in balance. It will cause him to sin and eventually bring chaos in that person as well as his surroundings, for the person of excessiveness targeted by the demon falls, and the demon destroys the room for the Word and the Holy Spirit to work, and without that room, there is no life. There will be no hope for him unless he turns to God, repents, and proves repentance by living in Jesus Christ.

Anyone who is in Jesus Christ will be a new creation, even the worst sinner; the old has gone, the one has come. (2 Corinthians 5:17)

The Word and the Holy Spirit in Jesus Christ will terminate Satan's work to tempt man to be in any excess.

Amazing Grace

John 3:16
"For God so loved the world that He gave His one and only Son, that whoever believes in Him shall not perish but have eternal life."

2 Corinthians 5:17-19
"Therefore, if anyone is Christ, he is a new creation..."

The old one has gone. The new one has come. All this is from God, that God was reconciling the world in Himself in Christ, not counting mankind's sin against them. Regardless of who he is, the poor, the rich, Jews or gentiles, anyone who is in Christ has salvation.

What an amazing grace of God!

It is too self-evident and too gracious to be feigned, because of presently imminent and visible things of this world, rooted in man's sinful nature, which blinds invisible immortal eternity.

Psalms 51:16-17
The Sacrifice of God

"You do not delight in sacrifice, or I would bring it; you do not take pleasure in burnt offering. The sacrifices of God are a broken spirit; a broken and contrite heart."

As said in Psalms 50:8-14, God does not ask for sacrifice for His needs, but to have the Israelites realize the obedience to His command.

The sacrifice of God is the sinners' groaning repentance of being contrite, and the broken heart from a broken spirit, which is a fragrance pleasing to God. God does not take pleasure in smelling burning animal fat or the murder of innocent animals. (Isaiah 66:3)

Romans 12:1-2
"Therefore, I urge you, brother, in view of God's mercy, to offer your body as a living sacrifice, holy and pleasing to God. Do not conform any longer to the pattern of their world, but be transformed renewing of your mind."

Paul urges to offer your body as a living sacrifice by putting to death whatever belongs to your earthly nature: sexuality, immorality, impurity, lust, evil desire, and greed. (Colossians 3:5)

All these are the products of man's sinful nature when it is triggered by Satan's temptation.

Therefore the absolute sacrifice, on top of others, is the soul and body redeemed by the Word and the Holy Spirit, burning away and washing away the products of sinful nature, which is man's seminal sin.

Redemption of the Body

The power of God works with mercy through Jesus' sufferings, showing what is the ransom of the believer to God, so that the believer may give the right ransom to God, which is the fat portions (man's sinful nature) which Abel offered to God.

When it is burnt away on the altar by fire and it is burnt away in man's heart by the fire of the Word and the Holy Spirit that comes from sorrowful repentance of a broken and contrite heart, the believer's body of the redemption becomes a living sacrifice, holy and pleasing to God. (Romans 12:1) If by the Spirit you put to death the misdeeds of the body, you will live, because those who are led by the Spirit of God are sons of God. (Romans 8:13-14)

Redemption of the body is the resurrection in Jesus Christ, being accepted as children of God for the kingdom of God to eternal life.

In two phenomenal events,
God allowed Satan to test and tempt man.

In The Old Testament, in Job1:12, 2:6

The Lord said to Satan, "Very well, then, everything he has in your hands, but on the man himself do not lay a finger."

The Lord said Satan, "Very well, then, he is in your hands, but you must spare his life."

With God's permission, Satan inflicted cruel and persistent sufferings on Job, only miserably sparing his life. Job must have been born of God, but he was not with the Word and the Holy Spirit, which caused him to be rebuked by God. "Who is this that darkens my counsel with the words without knowledge," He said, against Job's petition to God from out of his limit of patience (understanding of God's will), which coincided with the necessity that God planned to send the Son of the Word and the Holy Spirit for His plan for man's salvation.

In the New Testament, Matthew 4:1-1 says, "Then Jesus was led by the Spirit into the desert to be tempted by the devil."

This event is Jesus' triumph over Satan's tenacious temptations, with the Word and the Spirit who led Him into desert and was with Him throughout the temptation. Through this event, God clarified to destroy the work of Satan with the Word and the Holy Spirit as indicated in Ephesians 6:7, "the Word of the Spirit which is the Word of God," and John 17:17, "Sanctify them by the truth; your Word is truth," and John 6:63 "The Spirit gives life, the flesh counts for nothing. The Word I have spoken to you are Spirit and they are life."

God confirmed the end of the work of Satan with the Word and the Holy Spirit, which is the backbone of God's salvation plan for man.

Note: Genesis 3:4-7

Satan initiated the temptation of the first man by employing the crafty serpent to entice the first man, which opened Satan's fatal struggle against God's salvation plan for man (Genesis 3:15) according to God's plan.

Who put the fat portion (man's seminal sin) in man's heart?

Genesis 3:6

Good for food –unquenched greed

Pleasing to the eye–sensual lust

Desire—replacing God, the Creator, with the worldly gods of the age, their idols in their hearts, loving them more than the Creator.

Genesis 4:4

The fat portion which Abel brought represents man's seminal sins, termed into the sinful nature in the New Testament.

Leviticus 3:16

All fat portion is the Lord's. It must have been burnt away by fire, as the sinful nature by the Word and the Holy Spirit (Luke 3:16)

Psalms 51:5

David's confession for man's seminal sins: "Sinful from the time my mother conceived me."

Who put the fat portion (man's seminal sins) in man's heart? A significant clue can be found in Leviticus 3:16, "All fat is the Lord's," and 2 Corinthians 5:17-19, "If anyone is in Jesus Christ, he is a new creation." God was reconciling the world to Himself in Christ, not counting man's sin against them.

God the Omniscient must have been aware that the first man would fall at Satan's temptation, because "All fat portion is mine" is the beginning to open the chapter of man's salvation plan.

The beginning of faith and offering for man's sin
(Hebrews 11:14-31)

By faith Abel offered the fat portion of lust, greed, and evil desires with which Adam and Eve fell at devil's temptation.

God's salvation plan is through faith in Jesus Christ and in the power of God who raised Jesus Christ from the dead who was crucified on behalf of man's sin. The faith is to be traced from Abel's offering.

By faith Abel was revealed by God to offer him for the sin his parents had committed. Abel must have well been convinced that the offering should have been for atonement of the first man's sin, which is the first offering by faith for man's sin, the beginning of faith and offering for man's sin.

God's Probation to Man

Genesis 3:19

"God said, 'By the sweat of your brow, you will eat your foods..'"

One of the most irreversible dilemmas is that man has not observed the probation of God. On the contrary, man has sought to avoid this probation with every effort at the maximum in every field before the probation will be lifted by the work of the Word and the Holy Spirit, through which He has planned to save man, like stock investments making money without sweat, making robots, and eliminating human labor through computerization as much as possible for the same purpose, which

The purpose to avoid the probation "by the sweat of your brow" has been pervasive throughout human history and is beyond our control now.

God is accountable for the creation of man in His likeness.
That is His master plan, related to man's salvation.
The Lord God always acts in righteousness and justice.
He is righteous (Psalms 89:14, 145:17; Jeremiah 9:24)

According to His righteousness and justice, He came on the earth with the Word and the Holy Spirit through Jesus Christ, taking on a human body in the likeness of sinful man for the sacrifice of atonement for man's sin, which is the mystery. The mystery can be traced from His creation of man only in the likeness of Him, leaving the seminal sinful nature of lust, greed, and evil desires, which was tempted by Satan and caused the fall. (Genesis 3:6)

Here is a clue. His fatal opponent is Satan, from the beginning, as seen in Genesis 3:4-5, Job 1:8-12,Matthew 4:4-10, and how to destroy him is His absolute top target (1 John 3:8),which has an inseparable relation to man's salvation: destroying him with "neither might nor power but with my Spirit." (Zechariah 6:4) God's plan to destroy Satan is with the Word and the Holy Spirit through Jesus Christ from man who was created only in the likeness of God in righteousness and holiness, which is vulnerable to Satan's temptation.

God's righteousness and justice: "Therefore, if anyone is in Jesus Christ, he is a new creation; the old one has gone, the new one has come, all this is from God not counting men's sin against them." (2 Corinthians 5:17-19)

However, anyone who is in Jesus Christ should take off the old self and put on tge new self by sharing Jesus' sufferings becoming like Him in his death (Philippians 3:10-11, Colossians 2:11-12) by burying with Him through baptism into death (Romans 6:4).

God punishes everyone He accepts as a son (Hebrews 12:6) and removes all his impurities and all his idols thus making him clean by sprinkling clean water on him (Ezekiel 36:25) to become holy, because He is Holy.

His accountability for His master plan to destroy Satan from man with the Word and the Holy Spirit through Jesus Christ has been successfully ongoing according to His righteousness and justice.

"Glory to God"
"Thanks be to God"

One's life may be described as a long accumulation of habits, good or bad. Each of us is getting to learn habits and keep doing (repeating) them until he ceases his last breath. It will be blessed for him to say even at his last breath in spirit,

"Glory to God," and "Thanks be to God"
as the habit he used to express from the bottom of the heart in his daily
life ever since he learned and acknowledged them.
-Through your circumstances, wherever you are situated in this world—
rich, poor, high or low, in trouble or doing well, etc.,—God the Father
Almighty is to be glorified, for all things He created are nothing but the
instruments through which believers are to achieve our resurrection in
Jesus Christ for the Kingdom of God, the eternal life.

What Is the Ransom to God

As Jesus Christ's sacrificial atonement to God for man's sin is His
death on the Cross, so is the believers' putting to death man's sinful
nature (fat portion) and its practices with fire and power of the Word
and the Holy Spirit, and offering men's bodies, as well as their souls,
holy and pleasing to God. (Romans12:1)
-The gospel of the grace of God is not a list of rules to do this, and
we are not do do it for self-justification. Resources from God to make
radical change to the old self and transform mankind's inherent sinful
nature, body, and behaviors through the Word and this Sprit so that
believers may attain to the resurrection in Jesus Christ for the Kingdom
of God, sharing this grace of God with the world.
-Unless believers crucify the sinful nature and its practices through the
Word and the Holy Spirit, God, the Father may not receive us because,
He is holy and showed himself to us how to be holy through Jesus
Christ. (John 17:17-19)
Purify your soul by putting to death those idolatries; sexual immorality, impurity, lust, evil desires and greed (Colossians 3:5) as you
do with your body by burning fat with exercise every day. Burn these
idolatries with fire and the power of the Word and the Holy Spirit
every day.

-The modern faith

We make the mistake of excessive indulgence in the products of our sinful nature: love of money, sexual immorality, selfishness, evil desires, and all kinds of technology, etc., as if they will last forever, whether knowingly or unknowingly.

-The hope of believers in this world is redemption of the body as well as the soul.

-As Jesus Christ became the Son of God by His resurrection through the power of the Spirit, so His believers also become children of God by their resurrection in Him.

A Stranger

Genesis 3:23
"So the Lord God banished him from the Garden of Eden to work the ground from which he had been taken."

There are people who consider themselves to be strangers in the world, from their deep insight or just religious teaching. But to Christians, "a stranger" is to be differentiated from those people, since man was banished by God from the home of the kingdom of Garden, and became a stranger on earth. (Psalms 119:19) According to God's salvation plan to lift up the probation ("banished to the ground"), He sent the Word and the Holy Spirit through Jesus Christ; God sent the navigation to His lost peoples through Jesus Christ, which is the Word of God.

Man is to follow directions of the navigation in order to reach the final destination.

These are the scriptures mentioning "a stranger," and some supporting its meaning:

1 Peter 1:17

"Since you call on a Father who judges each man's work impartially, live your lives as a stranger." "Realizing that all men are like grass and all their glory is like the flowers of the field; the grass withers and the flowers fall, but the Word of God stands forever." (1 Peter 1:24:25. "… Which comes from having been born again, not of perishable seed, but of imperishable, through the living and enduring Word of God." (1 Peter 1:23) "…which enables man to purify himself by obeying the truth so that he loves one another deeply from the heart," (1 Peter 1:22), and also to love "the Lord your God with all your heart and with all your soul and with all your mind." (Matthew 22:37

"The time is short, for the world in its present form is passing away. Therefore those who are using the things in the world should do everything as if not engrossed in them." 1 Corinthians 7:29-32)

Jesus Christ showed us Himself as a model of stranger, as said in Luke 12:32-34.

A stranger lives his life not to possess but to be free from "mine," which means sharing with neighbors who are in need whatever he gains from this world through the talents the Creator has given to him. His load on the back is to be light to move freely as the Spirit of God leads him to eternity.

1 John 2:17

"The world and its desires pass away, but the man who does the will of God lives forever."

The will of God is the Word.

The Word of God is the navigation for a stranger through which he can return to the home of the kingdom of God to be with God in eternity.

Supporting Scriptures:

John 3:3-5

1 Peter 1:15:16

Colossians 3:5 & 8-11

Ephesians 5:3-5

Galatians 5:19:21 & 5:14

1 Thessalonians 4:7-8 & 4-3

2 Corinthians 7:1

1 John 2:15

1 Titus 6:10

Philippians 4:12

Romans 12:15-21

Mark 8:36-37

The New Covenant

Luke 22:20

"This cup is the new covenant in my blood, which is poured out for you."

Jeremiah 31:31-34

"When I make the new covenant, I will put my law in their minds and write it on their heart. For I will forgive their wickedness and will remember their sin no more."

The New Testament is the new covenant of Jesus Christ which involves His teaching, faith in His birth and death and the work of the Spirit, through which believers attain to the resurrection in Jesus Christ's resurrection for the kingdom of God.

Through the faith in the blood of Jesus Christ for the sacrifice atonement for man's sin, the Holy Spirit puts the Word of God in the believer's mind and writes it on their hearts, not on the tablet of stone, not by the hands of man but by Jesus Christ through the Holy Spirit of God who forgives all sins, redeeming the believer's life from mud and pits, removing all impurities and all idols.

"Blessed are they whose transgressions are forgiven, whose sins are covered. blessed is the man whose sin the Lord will never count against him." (Romans 4:7-8)

Everyone in Jesus Christ is A new creation. The old has gone and the new has come. This is the New Covenant through Jesus Christ.

Chapter 11

EPILOGUE

Romans 8:13-14
(By the Spirit)

"…but, if by the Spirit you put to death, the misdeeds of body, you will live, because those who are led by the Spirit of God are sons of God."

The only way to live by the Spirit is to be born again.

Unless man is born again, man cannot be led by the Spirit, because only the man born of the Spirit can be led by the Spirit of God.

Living in and being led by the Spirit produces the fruits of the Spirit: love, joy, peace, patience, kindness, goodness, faithfulness, and self-control (Galatians 5:22) through which man can taste the kingdom of God in the present world.

Glory to God who seeks, forgives, and saves the worst of sinners through the power of the Spirit, only if he repents, turns to God, and proves his repentance by living.

9 781977 243843